TEARS *and* LAUGHTER

One Man's Journey
through
Thirty Years Policing

By
David Griffin

authorHOUSE®

AuthorHouse™
1663 Liberty Drive
Bloomington, IN 47403
www.authorhouse.com
Phone: 1-800-839-8640

First published by AuthorHouse 01/11/2011

ISBN: 978-1-4567-7285-7

The cover picture is reproduced with kind permission from:
Im@gine Studio
29 Chester Road
Ellesmere Port
Cheshire

England

Printed in the United States of America

This book is printed on acid-free paper.

Dedication:

For Margaret and Don

Confidentiality:

Wherever possible I have used real names in telling this story. There are, however, some occasions when it has been necessary to change names and locations in order to protect privacy and confidentiality.

Acknowledgments:

Many people encouraged me to write this memoir, and for their support and encouragement I am very grateful. Particular thanks go to my wife Sally, Margaret Murphy, Mike Jardine and Jim Ronayne. I would also like to thank all those mentioned in the book, without whom I would have no story to tell.

David Griffin

December 2010

<u>Prologue</u>

Spring 1993

I rested the muzzle of the Heckler and Koch MP5 between the forked branches of the tree and surveyed the rear of the house. Some fifteen metres of garden lay between me and the back door. "In position with visual on the black face," I said into my radio mouthpiece. "Clear, unobstructed view from fifteen, one five, metres behind bulletproof cover. All quiet. Over." I checked the view through the telescopic sight on my weapon and stroked the safety catch with my thumb, as I had done many times when we practised these drills during tactical training sessions. This, however, was no training exercise. Inside the house was a man drunk on whisky and armed with a 9 mm self-loading pistol, believed to be Argentine army issue. Also in the house was an eight-year-old boy, the son of the man's girlfriend, who was being held hostage.

The hostage taker was a former soldier who had seen action in the Falklands War, so we could not afford to underestimate his ability with a hand gun. Having been involved in some of the most bitter fighting of the conflict, he had gone on to suffer bouts of depression and chronic alcoholism for a number of years before meeting the boy's mother. They had set up home together, and all the signs were that he was getting his life back on track – until he again lapsed into drink-fuelled depression and unpredictable behaviour. That day, having drunk a bottle of Scotch, he had produced the pistol and threatened his partner with it. As she ran from the house, he had grabbed her young son and threatened to kill him unless she returned. We were now more than two hours into the incident, and it had settled into a stand-off. After evacuating neighbouring homes, we had placed a containment around the property, and a police negotiator was in telephone contact with the man. The desired outcome was the release of the boy and the surrender of the offender, but this didn't look like it was going to happen any time soon.

He had continued drinking, was becoming more confrontational, and seemed fully prepared for a face-off. It was a dynamic, ever changing situation, and we had already drawn up a contingency plan involving a rapid, armed entry to release the boy. For now, though, we were prepared to play a waiting game in the hope that sense would eventually prevail.

The sun shone down from a cloudless sky even though summer was still some weeks away. Forced to sacrifice shade for cover and wearing heavy Kevlar body armour, I ended up soaked in sweat from head to toe. This was a distraction that I could well have done without because I could not afford to lose concentration, not even for an instant. Although only my head was exposed above the fork of the branches, the gun man could position himself at a window, get a good sight picture, and put a round through my face. I scanned the scene slowly and deliberately as I considered my options and rehearsed my responses to any contact situation. From previous experience I knew that the key to containing an armed suspect in a building was to stay switched on and not to give in to boredom or fatigue. Even a momentary lapse in concentration can prove disastrous, possibly fatal. Everyone had his own special way of staying alert during these often protracted operations; my technique was to allow myself to become slightly detached from the action and let a part of my brain to go about its normal business, while the rest of me remained firmly focussed on the job. On that spring day the free part of my brain was enjoying a flight of fancy when I was jolted back to reality by events unfolding inside the house.

I looked through the kitchen window, and my heart missed a beat. An internal door slowly opened, and a man walked into my view. White male, late thirties, five feet ten inches, slim build, cropped grey hair wearing a white T-shirt. This was him.

Was this it? Was this the moment?

I released the safety catch on the MP5, pressed my eye socket against the telescopic sight, and placed my finger against the trigger. He looked directly at me, remaining motionless with both arms at his sides. Through the scope his facial expression was clear; the red dot of my sight in the middle of his forehead. I could not see the boy, nor was a weapon visible.

"Visual contact with X-ray on the black face at one one," I whispered into my mouthpiece. *No weapon visible. No hostage in view. No immediate threat to public, colleagues, or me. Don't shoot.* In my mind I went through the drills practised many times during training.

It seemed like an eternity, but was probably less than a

3

minute, before the gunman walked out of the kitchen and out of my view.

I reapplied the safety catch and relaxed my grip, breathing heavily through my mouth. During training we had always been told to continue breathing during a contact situation. This seems like unnecessary advice, but there is a tendency to hold one's breath under these circumstances, and that was precisely what I had done.

"X-ray now out of view. Any sightings on the white face? Over."

Before anyone could reply, the man reappeared, this time at another window.

"Visual contact with X-ray on the black face at one three," I whispered. "Yankee also in view. No weapon visible. Stand by."

The window frame in this room was lower, and I could see him from the waist upwards, both arms still at his sides. I could also see the head and shoulders of the boy, and as I watched, the gun man placed his left arm around the boy's shoulder. I could not be certain, but I strongly suspected that the pistol was in his right hand. Assuming I was correct, he still posed no real threat to me. The chances of him being able to fire an accurate shot at me before I could squeeze the trigger were slim. He did, however, pose a very real and immediate threat to the boy. I had not joined the police to kill a man, but ultimately the life of the hostage is of paramount importance. Just a few weeks previously, other members of the team had shot a man dead in similar circumstances, so I was under no illusions about the seriousness of the situation.

Once again, I pressed my eye socket against the scope and released the safety catch.

This was it. This was the moment.

I placed my finger against the trigger and prepared to take a man's life.

<u>CHAPTER 1</u>

The Journey Begins

7 March 1977 – Cheshire Constabulary Training Centre, Crewe.

"Tutior Quo Paratior." That's what it said on the wall outside the Force Training Centre. As a product of the Catholic education system, I was not entirely unfamiliar with Latin, but this was a new one on me. Something to do with tropical birds, perhaps?

It was 8:30 a.m., one and a half hours earlier than the 10:00 start detailed in my joining instructions, and I wasn't entirely sure that the place was open. *Still, better to be in good time,* I thought as I approached the double glass doors through which I could see a Union Jack hanging limply from a brass pole. I pushed against the door and was half surprised when it opened. Walking somewhat nervously inside, I saw a large reception desk, behind which stood a police officer busily writing in a huge hardback book. As I approached the desk, I became aware of someone in my peripheral vision, and I turned to see another uniformed policeman standing some yards away, watching me with what felt like utter contempt. I guessed, correctly, that he was my reception committee and walked towards him, smiling inanely. The smile was not returned.

This individual was clearly identifiable as a drill instructor, in full mating plumage. Cap with peak severely slashed military style, best dress uniform with red diagonal sash and bulled boots, the toecaps of which dazzled with a mirrorlike reflection. Under his left arm he carried a wooden pace stick, and on his left breast he wore a name badge identifying him as Constable Adrian Lindop. After a Mexican stand-off lasting some while, I said, "David Griffin – This is my first day" and offered my outstretched hand. PC Lindop continued to stare at me from beneath his slashed peak for some time before producing a clipboard from a briefcase at his feet. He studied the clipboard for a second or two and then fixed me with a stare which was clearly not designed to put me at my ease.

"One thousand and two," he said.

"Sorry?" I replied, thoroughly confused.

"Why? What have you done?" he said, leaning towards me until our noses almost touched.

"Nothing," I said. "I just don't know what you mean."

"That's your collar number. One thousand and two."

I thought about replying, "I'm not a number. I'm a free man!" but I decided against it.

"Check in at reception, get your kit squared away in your room, and get yourself to the lecture theatre for 10:15."

"Where's the lecture theatre?" I asked.

"Read your joining instructions. You can read, I assume," he replied.

As warm welcomes go, this was right up there.

I walked over to the desk where the constable was putting the finishing touches to his entry in the big book.

"I'm Dave Griffin. One thousand and two."

This chap was an altogether different proposition from Mr Lindop, and he returned my smile with interest, slamming the big book shut before handing me a door key attached to a heavy metal fob.

"C23, fourth floor, west wing," he said. "Just follow the signs. Good Luck."

"Thanks, mate – Tutior Quo Paratior," I replied.

The force training centre, or FTC as it was known, was a converted nineteenth-century convent and grade two listed building. The frontage was an imposing five-storey edifice which housed the administration offices and classrooms. Onto the rear of this had been grafted the accommodation block, a rather incongruous 1960s glass-and-steel affair which gave the whole complex something of a university campus feel. Behind that were the playing fields, garages, and a small parade square where we would learn the rudiments of drill. On that bright, early spring morning in 1977, it seemed a rather pleasant place and not in the least intimidating, despite the best efforts of PC Lindop.

Having made my way to my room, I was surprised at how well appointed it was. Carpeted and centrally heated with built in wardrobes and wash basin, this was not the boot camp barrack room which I had expected. On the single bed was a sumptuous duvet, or continental quilt as they were rather quaintly known in those days. I had read of these things in *Ideal Home* magazine and was aware that they were the cutting edge of sleep technology – warm and cosy in winter, cool and light in summer. I looked out my window and had a panoramic view of Crewe, which although not up there with the great cityscapes of Europe, looked impressive enough to warrant a contented sigh.

I began to unpack my things as I considered the journey on which I was about to embark. My knowledge of the police service was limited to TV and film drama, but my motivation was strong, and I felt that I had made a sound career choice. Throughout my school years I had a well-developed sense of right and wrong, and now I would have a chance to uphold those values and to defend society against the bad guys. That's not to say that I had always been an angel in my youth; like all young boys, I had had my moments of rebelliousness and had got into one or two scrapes. I vividly remember one particular chemistry class when I had used a blazing Bunsen burner to set light to the teacher's white coat while he was wearing it. This incident had earned me legendary status among my peers but was rather less well received at home. The look on my mother's face when she read the letter from the headmaster is a memory that will stay with me forever, and technically I'm still grounded. But all that was in the past, and I was now about to become an officer of the Cheshire Constabulary. I was already starting to feel like some kind of comic book hero, ready to put myself in harm's way to prevent the destruction of civilisation as we know it. I lay on the bed imagining what excitement lay ahead for me when a glance at my watch indicated that I had just five minutes to get myself to the lecture theatre.

Having arrived one and a half hours early, I was now in serious danger of being late for my first appointment on day one of my service.

I burst into the lecture theatre with seconds to spare, nearly colliding with PC Lindop. He fixed me with that same icy stare which had greeted me on my arrival. A group of around twenty or so people were milling around the small theatre; some formed up into groups chatting in hushed tones. I saw two faces which I recognized from our meeting at Headquarters, Chester, some months before. Ron, Bill, and I had met that day when we took the entrants' exam and had later adjourned to a local pub for a debrief. Strangely, it had never occurred to me that we would meet again, but here we were, so I made my way over and shook their hands. Before we had chance to exchange pleasantries, PC Lindop had mounted the small stage to the front of us and attracted our attention with an ear piercing shout of "Right!" We were told to sit down, shut up, and listen in. PC Lindop stood to one side of the stage, ram rod straight with his pace stick under his arm. On the wall behind him was a large Cheshire Police badge. To the side of him was a wooden dais, on which he placed his cap and pace stick. He told us that Inspector Roberts and Sergeant Jackson would soon be joining us and that when they arrived, we would be told to stand up. He further told us that the Inspector, and indeed any officer of that rank or above, would be addressed as "Sir". Under no circumstances would we address a senior officer as Boss, Gaffer, or Guv, and we were never to even contemplate using a senior officer's first name, on or off duty. Equally, Sergeant Jackson was to be addressed as Sergeant, not Sarge or any other slang we may have heard on TV. "You will address me as Constable, or Mr Lindop," he told us.

At that, the door behind us opened, and in walked the Inspector and the Sergeant. "Room 'shun!" shouted PC Lindop, and the assembled mass stood up with varying degrees of enthusiasm and velocity. The ex-military types were immediately obvious by their speed and deportment, while some of the others were clearly unused to this kind of thing. The Inspector took up a position behind the dais, flanked by the Sergeant and Lindop, and invited us to sit down. It wasn't until he used the term "ladies and gentlemen" that I realised that there were a handful of females amongst our number. Sexual equality had become a fact of life for the police service three years previously, and these female officers would train alongside us before being deployed to operational posts.

The Inspector welcomed us to FTC and to the police service in predictable but reassuring fashion and gave us an outline of what the coming months held in store for us. We would spend our first week here at FTC Crewe, where we would learn something of the history and traditions of the service. We would be taught how to wear and maintain our uniforms, and there would be some military style drilling. There would also be some physical work in the gym and around the streets of Crewe, "to blow off a few cobwebs" as he put it. We would then move on to basic training proper at the Regional Training Centre at Bruche, near Warrington. This was where we would learn law, practice, and procedure, as well as being taught many of the day-to-day skills required of a police officer. Bruche was where officers from police forces across the country attended the ten-week recruit training course – the first element of the two-year probationary period. He concluded his welcome with some inspiring words about the career which we had chosen. His speech went something like this.

There are far easier ways to make a living than this, make no mistake about that. You have chosen a path which will bring you into daily contact with many of life's trials, tribulations, and tragedies. You will witness, first-hand, behaviour which will test your faith in human nature and make you question why you wanted the job in the first place. You will be threatened, abused, criticised, maligned, and sometimes physically assaulted by people whom you may feel are not fit to lace your boots. You may even experience rejection by some of your former friends, who will accuse you of having changed and become a different person. You will be working long and unsocial hours, often tired, cold, and hungry, and even your family will not fully understand what you are going through when things start to get on top of you. This life which you have chosen is no soft option, and in the coming weeks and months some of you may decide that it's not for you. But those who choose to stay will become members of a unique family. Like all families, we will sometimes not see eye to eye, and we may fall out from time to time. But as a family member you will always be looked after and supported. Many of you, I hope, will remain with us for thirty years and go on to draw your pension. Some of you, I hope, will achieve senior rank, but all of you will remember these first days in your chosen career. This is the day you are taking that first step on a long, often arduous, but always interesting journey. Good luck.

These words made a profound impression on me at a time when my senses were being bombarded with new experiences. I felt motivated and inspired, reassured that this was for me. The Inspector and Sergeant left the lecture theatre, and PC Lindop led us to one of the many classrooms, where we spent the rest of the morning filling out and signing various forms.

Over lunch in the canteen, I renewed my friendship with Ron and Bill before returning to the classroom to conclude our fist day as members of Cheshire Constabulary. We were not yet police officers, however. That transition would take place the following day, when we would wear uniform for the first time and swear the oath of allegiance before a magistrate at the local law courts.

Being prepared brings greater safety. So that's what the Latin phrase meant – Tutior quo paratior. Nothing at all to do with birds of paradise. I was completely alone in the library at FTC, not even a librarian to tell me to shush. The room appeared to be two of the large classrooms converted into one big oblong, with windows on one side which overlooked the rooftops of some terraced houses. The selection of books was quite impressive and covered a wide range of topics. Inevitably, much of it was given over to subjects relating to police work, but there were also books covering travel, sport, leisure, and history. There was a large section devoted to politics, which adjoined a small, free-standing bookcase housing a selection of language courses. It was here that I had discovered the Latin dictionary which I sought. I replaced the book and plotted how best to impress people with my newly acquired knowledge.

I then turned my attention to a section marked "General Interest – Various Authors", where I stumbled across a copy of *Death in the Afternoon* by Ernest Hemingway. This was a reference book about bullfighting and seemed a rather strange inclusion in a police college library. Now, I had never seriously considered a career as a matador. During my last year at school I had several one-to-one sessions with the careers adviser, and bullfighting had never been mentioned, not even as a long shot. In his defence, opportunities to pursue this line of work were probably somewhat limited in Birkenhead. Despite this, I found the book strangely captivating. The Corrida de Toros was described in Hemingway's unique style, as were the lives and times of a generation of toreros from Spain and elsewhere. I have no idea why, but I decided to borrow this tatty little paperback to enjoy at my leisure, though I was unsure of the correct procedure. With no bespectacled librarian to carry out the administration, I assumed there must be some kind of do-it-yourself system in operation, somewhere to record details of books being borrowed, so I began a painstaking search. At one end of the room was a large wooden desk, a kind of oversized writing bureau with drawers and shelves, which looked quite promising. I felt strangely furtive as I opened the top left hand drawer and rummaged inside. The thought struck me that on day one of my police career, it would probably not be a good idea to be caught red-handed rifling through someone's desk in a deserted library. Furthermore, to offer the defence that I was merely attempting to borrow a book on the history of bullfighting would probably not secure my acquittal at Chester Crown Court. My fears were, however, immediately forgotten when I made an exciting discovery in the second drawer: a big book identical to the one I had seen the constable writing in that very morning. It had a blue, marble effect hardcover on with black lettering that announced it as an "Occurrence Book". Intrigued, I placed the book on top of the desk, blew away several years' worth of accumulated dust, and lifted the cover. Inside were handwritten entries detailing a series of everyday events at Crewe Police Station. Dated 1965, the incidents included road accidents, domestic disputes, burglaries, and a long and sorry tale about a dangerous dog which had caused mayhem at an otherwise peaceful village fête. The book had a unique smell which seemed to encapsulate the stories contained within its discoloured pages. Casting an exploratory nostril over the dangerous dog entry, I was convinced I could detect the unmistakeable aroma of wet fur, sweat, and saliva.

Having searched every nook and cranny of the bureau without success, I decided to take the book to reception. I made my way down to the foyer and spoke to the PC behind the desk, a red-faced, jovial kind of a chap with wild, curly grey hair.

"What's the drill for borrowing this from the library?" I asked, showing him the dog-eared paperback.

"Bullfighting?" he said. "Is that in case things don't work out here?"

He took my details, made a note of the book's library number, and handed me an orange-coloured raffle ticket.

"Enjoy the book, amigo," he said with a broad grin.

I felt refreshed and relaxed as I tucked into my full English breakfast the following morning. I had retired to my room around 9:30 the previous evening and had read about Juan Belmonte, one of the legends of the Spanish bullfight, before practising a couple of basic passes using my continental quilt as a cape. Bill and Ron joined me at the breakfast table, and we chatted excitedly over our eggs and bacon. It was nine months or so since we three had first met on that fateful morning in Chester, and I had known immediately that we would become firm friends. Originally from Bedford, Ron had moved to Chester to take up a job in printing before deciding on a change of direction and applying for the police. With his black hair and Gregory Peck moustache, he looked a little like the cockney spiv of popular fiction, an image further enhanced by his rapier wit and ready smile. Bill had travelled from North Wales to pursue his dream and took life rather more seriously. With his shock of mousey hair and boyish looks, he could have passed for a clergyman, a role which he did successfully pull off some years later when a drunken prisoner demanded to be given the last rites. Even at this early stage it was apparent that Bill was one of life's worriers, but for all that there was a chemistry between us three which would bind us together over the coming years.

The Cheshire countryside looked wonderful through the window of the coach taking us to headquarters in Chester. Even though it was still early spring, there was real warmth in the sunshine as it bathed those lush green fields. We were on our way to be fitted with our uniforms, and I for one felt like a small boy on a school outing. Everyone seemed in high spirits; even Lindop looked reasonably contented as our coach turned onto the car park of headquarters. The setting was breathtaking, on the edge of the city overlooking the race course and the River Dee. The building, however, was the sort of monstrosity which would later become something of a cause celebre for Prince Charles. Seven stories of prefabricated concrete and glass, festooned with radio aerials, it would have looked much more at home somewhere behind the iron curtain. Bizarrely, one gable end of this architectural car crash was decorated with an abstract concrete design which had won an award for artistic excellence. Whoever nominated the building for this accolade must surely have been having a laugh, and whoever awarded it was either in on the joke or knitting with one needle. For me, the only way to improve the aesthetic appeal of this abortion would involve the use of a three-ton metal ball.

We formed up at the rear of the building and were ushered in through a set of double doors which took us directly into the uniform stores. Some twenty of us crammed into the reception area in front of a small counter, behind which stood the store's manager, Stan, and his two female assistants. The first thing that struck me was the smell, a unique cocktail of starch, steam, and damp cotton. The lighting arrangements were somewhat odd too: dimmed, slightly atmospheric, and clearly inadequate for detailed or delicate work. Maybe the seamstresses wore miners' helmets when sewing on buttons and insignia. The whole place appeared to be stuck in a time warp, a sort of nineteenth-century gentlemen's outfitters untouched by the vulgarity of the modern world. Lindop exchanged pleasantries with Stan before we were invited, four at a time, through into the inner sanctum to be kitted out. I was among the first batch and followed Lindop through a heavy beaded curtain (the sort you might expect to see in an Amsterdam bordello) and into the fitting area. Uniforms hung on moveable rails in front of shelves housing rows of helmets wrapped in brown paper.

Stan chose me as his first customer and positioned me, arms outstretched, in a kind of crucifix position. He then produced a brand-new tape measure from inside his jacket pocket, removing the cellophane wrapper very carefully. As he was taking my neck, chest, and waist measurements, he explained the importance of replacing his tape measure with a new one at regular intervals, monthly at least. "They stretch, you see, and then you get false measurements." I wondered if this was a conversation he had regularly – monthly at least – or whether it was just because we were new recruits, and he was merely trying to relax us with his bedside manner. He then took a tunic from the rail at his side and, with a flourish which would not have disgraced that great matador Juan Belmonte, swung it cape like across my shoulders. I slipped my arms inside as Stan fastened the silver buttons and guided me towards a full length mirror. The fit was perfect, testimony to Stan's tape measure theory, and the transformation was startling. Despite my grey check trousers, the metamorphosis had begun, and I started to feel the part. One of the two ladies handed me a pair of uniform trousers and invited me to step inside a curtained cubicle. Again, the tape measure theory held good, and the thirty-two long required no alteration. As I checked my image in the mirror, Stan took a helmet from the shelf, removed the brown paper wrapping, and handed it to me. This iconic piece of headgear is an image of the British police service which would probably be recognised anywhere in the world, and it felt good as I placed it on my head. A few minutes later we emerged back through the brothel curtain with all our uniform and equipment contained in two large carrier bags.

The coach trip to Crewe Magistrates' Court was the first time we ventured out in our uniforms, and I felt very self-conscious. As we filed in through the large glass double doors, we looked every inch what we were, members of the public dressed as police officers. Contrary to what I had expected, it was business as usual at the court that afternoon, and the public area was packed. Witnesses, solicitors, defendants, and a handful of genuine coppers mingled and chatted in hushed tones. We were herded into a corner of the foyer near to a pair of heavy oak doors, where a court usher in long black gown stood guard.

The usher pushed one of the doors slightly ajar and peered inside. Through the narrow gap I could see the three magistrates seated behind an imposing wooden desk some considerable height above floor level. On the wall above them was an ornate coat of arms, the familiar lion and unicorn, and the motto "Honi soit qui mal y pense".

The centre magistrate, the chairman of the bench, was addressing a sorry-looking individual standing in the dock with head bowed. I was unable to hear what was being said, but it was clear that sentence was being handed down, and the mood was appropriately sombre. All at once, everyone stood up, and amid much shuffling of papers, the magistrates filed out of a door at the rear of the room. The usher allowed the heavy wooden door to close and took a step back. A second later, the defendant appeared through the doors to be greeted by what must have been his worst nightmare, around twenty uniformed police officers. He froze, a look of horror on his face, and then sprinted for the exit pursued by a red-faced, heavily perspiring solicitor.

With a gesture of his head, Lindop indicated for us to make our way into the court. The usher guided us to a pair of long wooden benches where we sat, each of us holding a piece of paper bearing the words of the oath of allegiance. The chairman of the bench of magistrates reappeared from the door at the rear of the court, and Lindop told us to stand. I suppose I was expecting some more stirring words, along similar lines to what we had heard from the Inspector, but none were forthcoming. Instead, Lindop began to read from the printed sheet and indicated for us to join in. In unison, we solemnly promised to maintain the Queen's peace and to uphold the law, in the office of constable, without fear or favour. And that was that.

In many ways it seemed something of an anti climax. We were, however, now sworn in as police officers – constables of the Cheshire Constabulary, able to exercise our powers anywhere in England or Wales, whether on or off duty. I wondered why these powers did not extend to Scotland, but I guessed that England and Wales would do for now.

The short coach trip back to FTC passed in total silence as I, and I suspect everyone else, pondered the morning's events. Back at the centre we were ushered into an office where we were photographed one at a time and presented with our warrant cards, thus completing the metamorphosis from civilian to police officer. Again, there was a noticeable lack of pomp and ceremony as we placed the cards in our pockets and made our way to the canteen for our evening meal.

Red, pink, red, blue, red, pink. Twenty points. Not bad. Not bad at all.

Being a half decent snooker player is said to be the sign of a misspent youth, so there must have been more to Bill then met the eye. Ron and I watched with awe as he swept to a convincing lead in our tripartite competition. The games room was in what used to be the attic of the old convent and had required all of our combined orienteering skills to find. It was a huge room, big enough to accommodate a five a side football pitch, and was home to two full-size snooker tables, both maintained in pristine condition. According to several authoritative sources, it was also home to a ghost – an elderly nun who would regularly put in an appearance in a doorway at the far end of the room. This doorway gave access to a set of stone stairs which were part of the original convent and had remained unchanged for over 150 years. During one of the many refurbishments, the stairs had been bricked up at the level below, so they led to nowhere. There had, over the years, been dozens of reported sightings of the nun by a whole host of ostensibly credible witnesses. Even Lindop had mentioned her during his introductory talk on day one. He didn't claim to have seen her himself, but he certainly wasn't dismissive about the story. Now, I've never bought into the whole haunting thing – I just don't get it. If there is some kind of afterlife, and if these spirits do routinely take up residence in historic buildings, what do they get out of frightening the living daylights out of people? Is it some kind of sport? Do they get together over a few beers and have a good laugh about it? In any event, I certainly don't think it's something that the sisters of mercy should be getting involved in. Basically, I believe that these things exist only in the minds of gullible people who have read too many silly stories and who have a need to brighten up their dull and boring lives. This was precisely what I was telling myself as I placed my snooker cue back in the wall mounted rack and dusted the chalk from the front of my shirt.

"I think I'll turn in now, busy day tomorrow," I said, glancing at my watch to see that the time was approaching midnight. There was no reply, and I knew before turning around that I was alone. I stood and surveyed the empty room for some seconds, wondering how Ron and Bill had managed to scarper so quickly and without a sound. This was one of those rooms which had that unique ability to change silence from a negative thing into something positive. Something tangible.

The silence wasn't merely a lack of sound, it was the presence of quiet – a sensation not just for the ears. Despite the high ceiling, there was no hint of an echo. The room seemed able to muffle noise, swallow it almost. I suddenly noticed how chilly it was and became aware of a strange, musty smell.

I began to appreciate how this room could be appealing to a ghost looking for somewhere to party. Indeed, if I were a poltergeist, this was exactly the kind of place where I would want to ply my trade. Having absolutely no wish to exchange late night pleasantries with Sister Superior, I then felt an overpowering urge to sprint for the door. Unwilling to give in to such silliness, however, I took off at a moderately brisk yet still dignified pace, which I maintained until the room was plunged into total darkness. I covered the last few yards at full tilt, guided by the dim light visible from underneath the door. I threw myself at the door and burst out into the corridor outside, colliding with PC Lindop for the second time in my brief police career.

It was he, not the phantom nun, who had turned out the lights, thinking that there was no one in the games room.

"You again. Griffin, isn't it?" he said.

"Yes, Mr Lindop. I've been playing snooker," I said, rather unnecessarily.

He gave me a look which said, "Alone? At midnight? Weird!"

It seemed that every time our paths crossed, I was hell bent on confirming his initial suspicion that I was a complete idiot. With a shake of the head, he continued on his rounds, leaving me outside the games room. I was determined to wait until he was out of sight before making my way back to the accommodation block – I may have been the bumbling buffoon that he thought I was, but I certainly wasn't frightened of long dead nuns with a penchant for billiards. Having allowed a decent interval after his departure, I made my way towards the staircase when I was stopped in my tracks by a very distinctive sound. From inside the empty games room I heard the unmistakeable click of ivory snooker balls in gentle collision.

Most of the great bullfighters have come from Andalusia, where the best bulls are raised and where the warm climate and Moorish blood have given the men a grace and indolence. So Ernest Hemingway reckons, anyway, chapter 18, page 234. I was making good progress with the book. I placed the paperback next to the sink and looked at my reflection in the mirror. Blue shirt, black tie, sharply pressed tunic and trousers. My parade boots sat proudly on the writing desk, their gleaming toecaps covered by a yellow duster to protect them from any potential mishaps. Outside my window the sun shone down from a cloudless azure sky – a perfect English spring morning.

Out on the parade square, PC Lindop stood chatting to one of the driving instructors as we formed up in three rows ready for inspection by Inspector Roberts. Our first formal parade was a fairly relaxed affair, with the Inspector handing out some fatherly advice on how best to achieve the razorlike creases in tunics and trousers, which would be expected by the end of week two. It was clear that some of our number had never used an iron in anger before and would have to buck their ideas up.

Next up was a spot of PT, so it was back to the rooms to change into polo shirts, shorts, and plimsolls. Lindop joined us on this first session, a gentle jog around Crewe followed by an hour in the gym. Again the pace was leisurely, but I suspected that the tempo would be upped during the coming weeks.

Ron and I chatted whilst waiting in the queue for our lunch.

Like me, Ron was rather surprised at the gentle pace of things and the general lack of any military style shouting and bawling. Even the threat that was Lindop had so far failed to materialise, although I suspected that he was being restrained by the Inspector, rather like a snarling dog being kept on a short leash. I suggested to Ron that we should not be lulled into a false sense of security by the laissez-faire regime which we had experienced so far. One of the older PCs working on the reception desk had taken great delight in telling me about what lay ahead.

"Don't be fooled, mate, this is Butlins. Wait till you get to Bruche," he had told me. "Different ball game there. The instructors will run you ragged. PT, swimming, drill, self-defence, and then there's all the studying. Weekly law exams, and if you get less than 70 per cent, they'll have you back in the evening."

If this had been meant to worry me, it had had precisely the opposite effect. I couldn't wait to get stuck in and begin training for real. The next few days passed with lightening speed, and Friday afternoon arrived in the blink of an eye. We were once again gathered together in the lecture theatre where, under the watchful eye of Lindop, Inspector Roberts addressed us in his unique, fatherly fashion and wished us luck at Bruche. After the Inspector's departure, Lindop spoke to us in a subtly different vein.

"The staff at Bruche have ten weeks to turn you lot into something resembling police officers. I have my doubts whether that's possible, and I suspect that this may be the last I see of some of you," he said, fixing me with a stare.

"Those of you who do make it back here will then face a further twenty months of training and assessment, both here and on division, before you will be confirmed as constables. So far, ladies and gentlemen, you have achieved absolutely nothing – just remember that. Unlike the Inspector, I'm not going to wish you luck. If you're relying on luck to get you through this, then you've made a bad choice. What will get you through is hard work and determination, although for some of you even that may not be enough. Now get yourselves off and get stuck in."

I felt that Lindop's words hit the right spot and that maybe there was more to this aggressive martinet than I'd given him credit for. The look he gave me as we filed out of the room did not, however, suggest that he was reconsidering his initial opinion of me.

CHAPTER 2

Gardener's World

Monday, 14 March 1977 – District Police Training Centre, Bruche

Bruche Training Centre was approached via a small residential cul-de-sac in this leafy suburb of Warrington. Completely surrounded by semidetached houses, it seemed an incongruous setting for one of the UK's largest police training facilities. At the far end of the road was a military style gatehouse with a red and white striped barrier guarded by a police officer in best uniform. I drove towards the barrier, lowered my window, and showed my warrant card. He checked my details against those recorded on a clipboard, and I was ushered through the barrier and directed to the recruits' car park. From there I was directed to the lecture theatre inside the main building. Bruche was very different from the FTC, much more austere and far less welcoming. The walk from the car park took me past a collection of grim-looking, prefabricated two-storey buildings which appeared to be classrooms. The internal roads all had names and road markings, exactly like those outside of the barrier and beyond the wire fence which enclosed my new home. There were even dummy pedestrian crossings and bizarre signs which gave the place a surreal feel, almost like a film set. The main building was a single-storey construction of brick, wood, and glass surrounded by a well-manicured lawn and a carefully tended garden. A group of five or six men in green uniforms were silently weeding the borders, and one of them looked in my direction. He had a kind of sad, hang dog expression and bore a striking resemblance to the actor John Wayne.

"Morning!" I said.

The man averted his gaze and silently returned to his horticultural duties, which seemed strange. I was to later find out that the gardeners were in fact convicted criminals serving terms of imprisonment. These were men who were nearing the end of substantial prison sentences and were being gradually reintegrated into society by being given work on the outside. Some had been convicted of the most serious offences, including murder, and had not tasted freedom for many years. They were, apparently, under strict instructions to keep to themselves and not get into conversation with the staff or recruits. Clearly, John was sticking to the script.

I made my way into the large, open reception area, which was packed with new recruits. I looked around for a familiar face but saw none, so I stood alone and silent, waiting for the day to unfold. The atmosphere was one of excited confusion, reminiscent of my first day at secondary school. I was now a grown man, of course, but still felt that same nervous anticipation which I had experienced as an eleven-year-old. I then heard a resonant, deep voice announce that we were to make our way into the adjoining lecture theatre. The voice belonged to Sergeant Harriman, who would be our drill instructor for the duration of the course. We filed into the theatre, and I sat and looked up at the elevated stage. There were around 120 recruits from a number of police forces in this intake, and we fell silent as Sgt Harriman took the stage. Like PC Lindop, Sgt Harriman's status as a drill instructor was clear from his turn out and deportment. Ramrod straight, immaculate uniform, red diagonal sash and pace stick under his arm, his military pedigree was obvious. His resounding north eastern accent carried to all four corners of the large room without the need to shout. He told us to check the lists on the notice board outside the theatre to find out which class we were in. He told us that whilst we were allowed off the centre in our free time, we should be very careful if visiting the town centre in the evening, particularly where pubs were concerned. There had been problems between recruits and local men, resulting in a number of assaults. One public house in particular warranted a special mention and was declared out of bounds.

"Under no circumstances are any of you to visit The Highwayman pub. This establishment has a long history of trouble, and several recruits have been assaulted there. If any of you are foolish enough to disregard this instruction, and the matter comes to the attention of the staff, you will be returned to your force to face disciplinary action. If you want to have a drink off centre, there's a pub called the Dog and Partridge a short walk from here where you'll be made very welcome."

I made my way back to the reception area and scanned one of the notice boards. There were eight classes, lettered A to I, and my name appeared under class I. My classmates were officers from Merseyside, Lancashire, Greater Manchester, West Yorkshire, Cumbria, and West Midlands. I was the only Cheshire officer, which disappointed me somewhat, but

I felt sure that I would soon make new friends. I made my way towards classroom C14, where I met my new colleagues. The organisation of the police service in this country is uniquely different from any other. There are forty-three police forces in England and Wales, each jointly funded by the relevant local authority and central government. London has two police forces, the Metropolitan Police and the City of London Police. The latter polices the smallest geographical area in the UK – just one square mile. This isn't just any old square mile, though. It is *the* Square Mile, the epicentre of the metropolis which houses all the major financial institutions and some of the most prestigious business addresses in the world. Scotland has its own policing set up, and then there are other specialist forces such as the British Transport Police, who are responsible for the country's rail network; the Ministry of Defence Police, who control armed forces establishments; and the Atomic Energy Constabulary, who police nuclear sites. There are other smaller forces such as the Royal Parks and Gardens Constabulary. All of these police forces enjoy a surprising degree of autonomy, free from political or governmental interference, and it is this freedom which is at the very heart of the British policing principle.

Our class instructor introduced himself as Sergeant Edwards, a Lancastrian serving with Merseyside Police. In his early forties with a brusque, no-nonsense style, I got the impression he would expect and demand high standards. The morning passed in a flurry of form filling before we made our way to the canteen for lunch, a rather uninspiring affair which had me yearning for the choice and quality which had been on offer at the FTC. Having had my fill of rubber sausages and some spectacularly tasteless objects rather exotically described as 'French style potato croquettes',

I poured myself a cup of coffee from one of the many steel pots which were placed at intervals along the narrow tables. I immediately smelled the proverbial rat when I saw that the coffee had milk already added, giving it a River Ganges hue. I decided to taste it before adding my normal spoonful of sugar, in case that chore had been thoughtfully taken care of as well. To convey the taste of this concoction through the medium of language is frankly beyond me. I had read somewhere that during World War Two, when coffee was in short supply, the Germans used to drink Ersatz coffee made from crushed acorns. The thought struck me that maybe there was an ex-prisoner of war employed in the kitchens and that he was keeping this fine tradition alive.

My room was bleak, bare, and unwelcoming, with none of the bourgeois decadence of the FTC. Sleep technology had evidently not yet reached this outpost of suburban Cheshire, and the continental quilt was conspicuous by its absence. In its place was a pale blue candlewick bedspread and starched linen sheets. There was a small writing desk, a chair, and a bedside cabinet which, together with a built-in wardrobe, completed my home comforts. A pair of faded blue curtains framed the small window which afforded an uninterrupted view of the recruits' car park. While I had been pleasantly surprised by the facilities at FTC, I found this place rather depressing. Still, mustn't grumble. I unpacked my things and changed into uniform for the afternoon. Unlike FTC, where pretty much everything was under one roof, this place was a collection of outbuildings. Whenever moving from one place to another, "helpful" staff members were on hand to give advice about dress and deportment. Also, anyone of inspector rank or above had to be saluted in correct, military fashion. From the next week onward, failure to recognize a senior officer or pay the appropriate salutation would result in punishment in the form of extra duties.

Sergeant Edwards spent the afternoon outlining exactly what the next ten weeks held in store for us and advising us of the many rules and regulations which would be rigidly adhered to. There were eighteen of us in the class, and it was clear that for some this was their first taste of a disciplined environment. I wondered if some of them would not be here for the passing out parade in the summer. Training would begin in earnest at 8:30 the following morning, but for now day one at Bruche was over. The Sergeant concluded with a reminder about the potential hazards of drinking in the town centre pubs in general and the Highwayman in particular. They really were making heavy weather of this establishment and clearly meant business when declaring it off limits. I had a mental picture of some lawless Klondike saloon during the gold rush, full of trigger-happy, dentally challenged desperadoes.

Told you once before and I won't tell you no more,
get down, get down, get down.
You're a bad dog baby, but I still want you around.

Gilbert O'Sullivan was in fine voice on the juke box at the Highwayman as Alfie and I sipped our cold beers, flicking dry roasted peanuts into the air, and caught them in our mouths – sometimes. He and I had met first an hour or so earlier in the bar at Bruche and had decided to sample, first-hand, the dolce vita that was Warrington by night. A stocky, bull-necked scouser serving with West Yorkshire Police, Alfie seemed like convivial company, and we had chatted like lifelong friends during the short walk. The

Highwayman proved something of a disappointment: light on atmosphere, not remotely menacing, and not a desperado in sight. An elderly man sat at one end of the bar reading his newspaper while two middle-aged women harangued the barman about how the place had gone downhill since the new landlord had taken over. The décor was badly in need of a little TLC, and the soft furnishings had that kind of sticky feel unique to rundown public houses. The ceiling was regulation Woodbine yellow, and the windows were opaque with years of grease and nicotine. All of this was at odds with the carpet, which was thick, sumptuous, and quite obviously new. The barman was stick thin with lank, greasy grey hair and a pointy, ferretlike nose. He wore a black leather waist coat over a sweat-stained T-shirt adorned with "Elvis – The King". He was telling the two women that the carpet was indeed new, had been laid just a few days previously, and was very expensive.

"Top quality Axminster, you know, wool and nylon. Nearly five hundred quids' worth," he announced with considerable pride.

It struck me as a bizarre extravagance to splash out that much on carpet when the rest of the place was such a complete toilet. *But at least the customers will be able to fight in comfort,* I thought. It was at this point that Elvis turned his attention to us.

"You're not regulars lads; where you from?"

Alfie was first out of the blocks with "Liverpool, mate – we're staying at a B&B up the road. We're bricklayers."

Cool! I thought. *Second week in the job and I'm undercover!*

"Thought you might have been coppers from that Bruche place," said the barman.

"Kidding, aren't you, mate?" replied Alfie. "Can't stand 'em."

"There's a gang of 'em in the lounge," said Elvis. "Good for business, but the locals hate them. We've had some problems, scraps and that, you know. Couple of weeks back it was like a Wild West saloon, three bizzies got a right smacking."

"Gets my vote," said Alfie, flicking and catching a dry roasted with consummate skill.

I peered through the frosted glass panel in the door and saw around a dozen of our colleagues sitting at a long table and chatting over their pints.

It was at this point that the door opened, and four heavily built men walked in and made their way to the pool table. Elvis began pulling four pints of Boddingtons Best Bitter.

"On the bar, Gary!" he shouted, and two of the men walked across, looking down at their feet and taking strange, catlike steps.

"What's this?" asked one of them, indicating the wool and nylon Axminster.

"Carpet, you knob. What's it look like?" said Elvis.

"Shite," was the reply.

As they picked up their pints, one of the men looked sideways towards me and gave me a look which suggested strangers were not welcome at this particular inn. The look wasn't so much one of menace, more of disgust – the way one might regard a freshly laid, steaming turd. I instinctively knew that a cheery smile and a "Turned out nice again" would not have been a good idea, so I fixed him with an unblinking stare which lasted for some seconds. This was something which I had done many times during my school days and was rather good at, if I say so myself.

They returned to the pool table and began setting up the balls and chalking the cues, all the time looking across at Alfie and me. We feigned disinterest and continued making small talk with Elvis. One of the men, a shaven-headed six footer with a fondness for tattoos, stared in our direction.

"Do us a bacon butty, will you, Catweazle!" he shouted. "Pronto."

"Coming right up, Sir," Elvis replied, winking at us.

"On second thoughts, forget that 'cos I don't like bacon – can't stand pigs," shouted our new friend. His three cronies began to roar with laughter before snorting like a gaggle of porkers.

Alfie put his pint down, stood up, and faced the four men. Everything was silent except for the sound of Elvis removing breakable objects from the bar. The old guy at the end of the bar closed his newspaper, sat back on his barstool, and folded his arms.

"You got a problem, donkey droppings?" inquired Alfie.

"You're pigs, aren't you?" the man replied.

"Police officers, actually – You're the pigs," replied Alfie.

"You speak for yourself, copper, I'm a bricklayer," I felt like shouting, but the cat was out of the bag now.

"How about a nightcap at the Dog and Partridge?" I whispered to Alfie, but he was already squaring up for battle. "Do you think this is a good idea, mate?"

"What they don't know is that we've got reinforcements

next door," he whispered with a smile, as he moved towards the pool table.

What Alfie didn't know was that the Seventh Cavalry had ridden out of town and could now be seen through the window some two hundred yards away, meandering back to the sanctuary of Bruche. I tapped him on the shoulder and pointed to our disappearing colleagues outside.

"Oh shit!" he said.

"Exit stage left!" I suggested, and we ran for the door chased by four very angry men.

The physical training of previous weeks soon paid dividends, and we quickly built up a comfortable lead on the pursuing pack. I even felt sufficiently confident to turn and flick a few V signs – probably not behaviour becoming of an officer of the law, but immensely satisfying none the less.

Sergeant Harriman marched across the parade square, stopped, and turned to face us, bringing his boot down onto the tarmac with a crack which sounded like a rifle shot. We were formed up in our eight classes, in ranks of three, with the relevant instructor standing to the front of each class.

"Parade! Parade ... 'Shun!' he shouted, and as one, we snapped to attention in the manner we had practised during the preceding week. The Deputy Commandant, a chief inspector of the Lancashire Constabulary, marched onto the square and was saluted by Harriman.

"Parade. Parade, stand at ... ease!"

We were then brought to attention again, class by class, to be inspected by the Deputy Commandant. This was our first parade at Bruche, so no one was berated for their turn out. This was, after all, only our eighth day as police officers.

Sgt Harriman brought us back to attention again before saluting the Chief Inspector, glancing over his left shoulder, and shouting, "Music, Maestro!" There then followed a rather comic moment as the introductory scratching sound of a well-used gramophone record echoed across the parade square. We were then treated to the stirring music of the Band of the Coldstream Guards, Harriman's old regiment, apparently. The piece of music was one which I immediately recognised, although I had no idea what its title was. I had heard my father sing it many times while gardening. It begins with the words, "Have you ever caught your bollocks in a rat trap?" These lyrics were, I suspect, not the original ones, but they were the words sung with much gusto by Dad and his comrades in the Lancashire Fusiliers during the Second World War. More than thirty years later, here I was proudly singing those same words, though only in my head, as we marched off the parade square and headed for the classroom.

The constable is a citizen. He is locally appointed and he derives his authority from the Crown. That was our first lesson, and the significance of those words is worthy of further explanation. Unlike virtually every other country in the world, the British police officer has very few powers which are not available to the general public. He or she is essentially an ordinary member of the public paid to perform a role which everyone else would be expected to perform as a matter of conscience. He is categorically not a member of the armed forces, as is the case in many other countries. Police officers are selected and appointed by the local police forces to which an individual chooses to apply, there being no national police force. Finally, the limited powers which a police officer does have are conferred by the Crown, not by the government. There is, therefore, no political control over policing in Britain. Much of the classroom work during those first few days at Bruche was devoted to exploring these principles of policing and how it was important to maintain the support of the public. It was only once we had grasped and understood these concepts that we moved on to law, practice, and procedure. Legal definitions, powers of entry, search and arrest were drummed into us, as were forensic and evidence-gathering techniques.

The morning parades were now an altogether more exacting experience. Those whose turn out failed to reach the high standards demanded by Sgt Harriman were given a very public dressing down and were assigned to extra duties during the evening. Extra duties were something to be avoided at all costs because free time was very limited. When the working day ended at 5:00 p.m., we filed into the canteen for rubber food, French potato croquettes, and acorn flavoured coffee.

Between 6:00 and 7:00 p.m. we were confined to our rooms for the quiet hour, to study the topics we had covered that day, and 7:00 to 9:00 p.m. was maintenance of uniform and equipment. Our only free time was between 9:00 and 11:00 p.m., when we could visit the bar in the main building or leave the centre. By 11:15 p.m. all recruits were obliged to be in their rooms, and lights out was at 11:30. Most of the administrative functions necessary for the running of the centre were carried out by the recruits, so on at least one evening each week the working day lasted from morning parade at 8:30 a.m. to lights out. These roles included perimeter security, reception desk duty, telephone exchange, bar duties, and a whole host of other activities at the discretion of the duty officer. Clearly, an extra helping of these duties was about as welcome as a lizard in the bidet.

Now, I'm the first to concede that pork scratchings are not everyone's cup of tea. Little bits of hairy, fleshy pig fat fried until they have a texture somewhere between wood and concrete, they are something of an acquired taste. After a couple of days of Bruche's cuisine, however, they are a culinary joy. On the wine front, a robust Pinot Noire or possibly even a hearty Rioja would be the perfect accompaniment. On this occasion, however, Ron, Bill, and I had opted for the Greenalls lager. The décor in the bar at Bruche was in keeping with the rest of the establishment: minimalist chic with wiped clean Formica very much in evidence. Rather like the interior of a working men's club, furnishings were sparse so as not to distract from the main business, drinking. A homely touch was provided by some yellowing lace curtains adorning the windows at the side of the room. On examination of these curtains, I noticed a series of small, perfectly circular holes at head height. These holes were in groups, almost as though someone had discharged a machine gun at the curtains, which seemed unlikely. I was intrigued by the holes and could think of no plausible scenario whereby this situation could arise. It was clear that they were not the result of ageing or general wear and tear. Equally, they were far too regular in shape to have been caused by hungry moths; also, although I know very little about the dietary habits of moths, I doubt that nylon is on the menu. Could they have been made deliberately, and if so, why? I asked a number of people if they knew anything about the holes, but no one was able to shed any light on the matter. What was even more significant was that no one else had ever noticed them before – nor was anyone remotely interested except me, and I was determined to get to the bottom of this mystery before the end of the course.

We had a lot of socialising to cram into two hours and were already on our fourth pint when I felt a tap on my shoulder and heard the words, "Pass us your empties, Griff." I glanced up to see Alfie, resplendent in maroon nylon jacket and armed with a plastic crate into which he was placing empty pint glasses.

"Doing a bit of moonlighting?" I asked.

"Not by choice, mate," he replied. "Went out last night and lost track of time. Got back at ten past eleven and got clobbered with extra duties. Two hours collecting bleeding glasses for the sake of ten minutes. I felt like Cinderella late back from the prince's ball."

"Well, rules are rules, Cinders," I said. "Now on your way, we've got drinking to do."

Alfie leaned towards me and whispered, "Fuck off."

I told Ron and Bill about the trip to the Highwayman and how Alfie and I had faced off a group of at least a dozen thugs who had left with their tails between their legs and a warning never to return. Okay, so I did exercise a little poetic licence, and I may have added the odd embellishment here and there, but it wasn't as if I was under oath.

Ron looked amused and impressed by the story; Bill was clearly horrified. With the time approaching 11:00, the Duty Sergeant put in an appearance at the bar, telling us to finish our drinks, and a few minutes later the national anthem was played over the tannoy system. We stood to attention and tried to look as serious and patriotic as is possible after four pints. Bill began to mouth the words whilst staring straight ahead. Ron and I looked at him, looked at each other, and began to lose our composure. To a sober man the words of the national anthem are not remotely amusing, but after four pints of lager they take on a whole new comic perspective.

"Send her victorious, happy and glorious," mimed Bill, as Ron and I struggled to hold back the laughter. Our high spirits had been spotted by the Duty Sergeant, a snarling, bulldog face type who clearly did not share our sense of fun. As soon as the music stopped we ran for the exit, where we were able to let the pent-up hilarity out before sprinting back to the accommodation block.

In the classrooms we learned about powers of stop and search, powers of arrest, and how to deal with offenders, witnesses, and victims of crime. Our newly acquired knowledge was regularly tested during practical role play sessions on the film set streets of the training centre. We would each take our turn dealing with incidents while the rest of the class looked on. The various roles were played by staff members who acted as villains, drunks, abused wives, irate shopkeepers, and mentally disturbed hospital patients. Some of them played these parts as proficiently as professional actors. One in particular, Sergeant Ernie Storr, was so convincing in the role of a violent drunk that it was hard to believe that he was acting. To add to believability of his performances, he had what on the West End stage would no doubt be described as an interesting face – part Sir Laurence Olivier, part Popeye. The contours of his visage appeared to be the result of numerous incidents of violent trauma, most probably caused by blunt instruments, and not the kinds of injuries likely to be sustained whilst flower arranging. Everything about the man, from his slightly bow-legged walk to the jaunty angle of his uniform cap, suggested that he was a graduate of the university of life. With fists the size of cabbages and the physique of a circus prize fighter, he was not the sort of man you would choose to get on the wrong side of. When taking part in the role play exercises, he would stagger, swear, throw punches, vomit, and urinate with such panache as would warrant a BAFTA nomination. The bodily fluids came from an assortment of plastic containers which he concealed under his clothing and were always discharged when he had his back to the recruit who was dealing with the incident. He was also able to fall backwards like a felled tree without injuring himself, usually when the poor recruit had just begun to take control of the situation. This was the cue to demonstrate our first aid skills, placing the casualty in the recovery position before checking pulse and breathing.

Like any thespian worth his salt, Sergeant Storr was determined not to be typecast and was by no means a one-trick pony. Amongst the staff at the centre he was known as the Smoking Dolphin, a reference to a unique trick which he would perform for each new intake of recruits. As chief swimming instructor he was responsible for ensuring that everyone qualified for the Bronze Medallion in life saving during the ten-week course. Considering some of the recruits arrived as nonswimmers, this was no easy task, and much of our time was spent in the pool learning the various techniques which would be tested for the award. During our first swimming session, he announced that he would perform the smoking dolphin trick when, and only when, he was satisfied that we had made good progress as a class. This was undoubtedly a sound psychological ploy and certainly encouraged endeavour, even among the handful of chlorine dodgers whose enthusiasm was questionable. Some four weeks into the course, we were formed up at the poolside when the Sergeant congratulated us on our progress and announced his intention to demonstrate his unique talent for us. He reached into the pocket of his tracksuit top and produced an untipped Capstan Full Strength cigarette and a Clipper lighter. With great showmanship he flicked the cigarette into the air and caught it between his lips. A ripple of applause was cut short by a dismissive wave of his hand and a facial expression which said, "You ain't seen nothin' yet!" He lit the cigarette and began to draw heavily on it, causing it to glow extravagantly and burn down very quickly. Whilst doing this he stripped down to a pair of black Speedo trunks and made his way to the deep end of the pool, where he stood to attention at the eight foot mark. Without using his hands he then deftly flicked the cigarette backwards so that he was gripping it between his lips but with the lit end inside his mouth. He puffed out his cheeks and blew a huge cloud of smoke from his nostrils, like an enraged dragon. Still standing to attention, he launched himself pencil like into the pool, immediately sinking to the bottom, before starting to walk along the pool floor towards the opposite side. After what seemed like an eternity, he hauled himself out at the opposite side of the pool, stood to attention, and flipped the cigarette back to the conventional position. It was clearly still alight and was soon producing clouds of smoke to the sound of thunderous applause from an appreciative audience. One of our number, a West Midlands officer named Wesley, did not join in the applause and looked strangely ill at ease with the performance. As a normally extrovert and gregarious character, this struck me as slightly odd but all became clear during our conversation in the changing room.

"What's up, Wes?" I asked.

"It's this Bronze Medallion thing. I don't think I'm going to get through it."

"Course you will. It's no big deal," I offered reassuringly.

"You don't understand, there's no way I'll pass that test"

"Why?" I asked.

"Well, as you know, I'm not the strongest swimmer. And I've never smoked in my life!"

Common law and statute law differ in that the former is not actually written down anywhere. Offences against common law tend to be those which are so patently wrong that society has never felt the need to pass acts of parliament forbidding them. Murder, therefore, is a common law offence whilst criminal deception is catered for within the Theft Act of 1968. Much of the studying at Bruche involved memorising the often complex definitions of offences and the relevant police powers to deal with them. The Victorians were very keen on statute law, and many of the acts of parliament which we had to commit to memory were written in nineteenth-century English. The time was approaching 9:00 p.m., and I sat thumbing through my copy of *Baker and Wilkie's General Police Duties* when I spotted a particularly bizarre piece of legislation. Apparently, it is a summary offence to cause or permit a servant to climb out onto a window ledge more than eight feet above street level for the purpose of cleaning a window. Considering health and safety was not high on the Victorian agenda, I found it odd that they had taken the trouble to pass an act of parliament outlawing this practice. It was not until I read the final line of the definition of the offence that I realised the well-being of the servant was not the issue here. The definition concludes with the words "to the danger or annoyance of residents or passengers". So that was it; the Victorian gentleman strolling arm in arm with his suitably corseted wife did not want his sojourn spoiled by some scruffy, working-class type crashing to his death in front of him. I can see how that would have been mildly annoying and could potentially ruin an otherwise pleasant evening. One can only assume that there was a time when this type of thing was commonplace, with many a relaxing promenade wrecked by falling servants. The always pragmatic Victorians addressed the issue by passing an act of parliament, and stiff upper lips were maintained. I suddenly felt very proud to be British.

Having initially dismissed *Baker and Wilkie's* as a boring textbook, I now discovered that it was a rich source of weird and wonderful nuggets of legislation. There were laws to prevent the beating of rugs between the hours of 10:00 p.m. and 8:00 a.m., the irresponsible disposal of barbed wire, the chiming of bells after dark, and a particular favourite of mine, showing a horse with gladding. For the uninitiated, let me explain. Gladding is an equine skin complaint which was apparently rife in the 1800s. This piece of legislation makes it an offence to take a shire horse suffering this affliction to any county fair or market with the intention of showing the animal. Punishable by a fine of ten shillings and/or twenty-eight days imprisonment, this was clearly something up with which Victorian sensibilities would not put.

The examination room was silent except for the ticking of the huge clock on the wall above the Sergeant's head. As the second hand reached twelve, we were instructed to open the exam paper and begin. Evidence, practice, and procedure in relation to crime, traffic, and general police duties – this was the final test of the ten-week recruits' initial training course, requiring a mark of 70 per cent. Those failing to reach the minimum mark would spend every evening of the following week as guests of the supplementary training unit before retaking the exam the following Monday. For anyone failing the retest, their police career would then be in the hands of the Chief Constable, who could either back class the individual or dismiss them. As I read the questions, I was disappointed not to see any questions about equine skin complaints or the unlawful beating of rugs. I picked up my pencil and began ticking the relevant boxes of the multiple choice questions. Each one had four possible answers, so there was a school of thought that even a chimpanzee would be likely to score 25 per cent by ticking boxes at random. Alfie was a leading exponent of the random ticking technique and had explained to me how one's score could be further increased by creating a certain pattern of diagonal lines across the answer sheet. He was adamant that his theory was based on a sound mathematical formula and that, if followed scrupulously, would guarantee a mark of between 70 and 80 per cent. Alfie had so much faith in his system that he had employed at each of the weekly progress checks throughout the preceding eight weeks. Sadly, he had been a student of the supplementary training unit for seven out of the eight weeks, having averaged around 35 per cent each time. The one week he did reach the pass mark was surrounded by controversy because he came top of the class with a score of 82 per cent. Wesley, who normally finished in top spot, failed that week with a score of 35 per cent. The smart money was on a mix-up of answer sheets, and the following week it was business as usual. Alfie, however, would have none of it and saw his success as vindication of his system. Despite Alfie's well-intentioned advice, I stuck to my strategy of reading the question, planning my response, and then looking for the option which most closely matched my answer. After two hours we had to down pencils, and that was that. I glanced across to Alfie, who held up his answer sheet showing me an impressive pattern of crosses and diagonal lines. He placed the sheet back on his desk, gave me a knowing wink, and sat back with his arms folded. He looked contented, relaxed, and sublimely confident. I somehow knew that he would be enjoying the hospitality of the supplementary training unit the following week.

What little time remained of the course was spent with further examinations in first aid, swimming, and self–defence, as well as practising complicated drill movements in preparation for the passing out parade. I approached this final week of initial training with excitement and sorrow in equal measure. I was greatly looking forward to hitting the streets and doing some real policing, but part of me was sad to be leaving this place, which had been my home for the last ten weeks.

The atmosphere in the bar was something special the evening before the passing out parade. Alfie was in high spirits, having scraped through the final exam after a week of intensive tuition in the supplementary training unit. He remained convinced of the infallibility of his system of intricate patterns where multiple choice answer papers were concerned, although he did concede that his technique needed some fine tuning. "The system applies just as well to the football pools. It's a foolproof mathematical formula – I've been using it for two years now" he announced with absolute confidence and not a hint of irony in his voice. Confident in the knowledge that Alfie would never land a life-changing win with Littlewoods, I somehow knew he would go on to make a first-class copper and that the people of West Yorkshire would benefit from his wit and wisdom.

I made a decision to mingle and chat to as many people as possible, knowing that this would be the last I ever saw of many of them. It was customary for the staff to share a drink with recruits on this last evening of the course, and when I saw Sgt Storr holding court on the far side of the room, I headed across to offer my thanks for his efforts during the preceding weeks. He was chatting to a small group of recruits and regaling them with stories of days gone by policing the streets of Manchester. As I approached, someone handed him a pint of beer. He transferred his double Scotch to his left hand, placed his Capstan Full Strength between his lips, and grasped the pint pot with a nod of gratitude.

It was at this point that I heard the sound of raised voices outside. Two recruits were arguing loudly and drunkenly just outside the window. It was impossible to hear exactly what was being said, but there was mention of a female class member, a seedy night club, and an incident in the bushes behind the duck pond. It was clear that intellectual debate had run its course and that punches were about to be thrown. This type of free entertainment was clearly to Sgt Storr's liking, and he was not about to miss out on the chance of a ringside seat. With a subtle nod of the head, he beckoned his little group closer to the window to enjoy the developing cabaret. As he leaned towards the yellowing lace curtain for a better view, it happened. The glowing red tip of his Capstan cigarette touched the nylon drape. There was a crackle, a fizz, and – voila! A small, perfectly formed circular hole identical in every respect to the dozens of others was created. So that was it! Sgt Storr was the culprit! He had single-handedly fashioned these wonderful circles which had fascinated me for the last three months. It felt like an omen. On the last evening before leaving this place forever, I had solved the mystery of the holes and could now move on. I would not have to spend the rest of my life wondering, agonising, hypothesising. The fist fight outside the window was suddenly of no interest to me, although Sgt Storr was clearly enjoying every minute of it. Shadow boxing with a whisky in one hand and a pint of bitter in the other cannot be easy, but Ernie Storr carried it off with style, and hardly a drop was spilled. The show was brought to a premature end by the Duty Sergeant, who delivered an impressive kick to the backside of one of the participants while grabbing the other one by the scruff of his neck. I wasn't entirely sure which technique from the officially sanctioned self-defence system he used, but it looked effective, and Sgt Storr nodded his approval.

The Union Flag fluttered gently above the parade ground on that perfect summer day in 1977. On the edge of the square a small stage had been constructed, complete with seating for the distinguished guests, including William Kelsall, Chief Constable of Cheshire. To the rear of the stage the band of the Cheshire Constabulary was formed up, ready to provide the music for the passing out parade. A crowd of around 250 friends and relatives of the recruits stood around the square, all dressed in their Sunday best. My wife, Mary, and my parents were somewhere in that gathering as I stood proudly to attention, staring straight ahead. The entire intake of around one hundred officers were formed up in class order, and after an inspection by Chief Constable Kelsall, we performed Continuity Drill. This was a complex set of drill movements performed without instructions and involved marching, stopping, turning, and saluting in a predetermined order. We had been practising this drill for many weeks, and Sgt Harriman was clearly proud and relieved when we completed it without error. We then marched off the square to the music of the Constabulary Band and the rapturous applause of the watching family members. There was hardly a dry eye as we halted outside the accommodation block. I've never been one for public displays of emotion, but even I felt strangely tearful that day. I reminded myself of the words of PC Lindop, that we were still a long way from being police officers and had achieved nothing as yet, but this somehow felt like an achievement, and I was proud.

CHAPTER 3

Reality Check

June 1977

Ellesmere Port Police Station is an unremarkable building in an unremarkable town. On this, my first day as an operational police officer, I had parked my car some distance away and walked through the town centre, feeling excitement and apprehension at what lay in store for me. Despite the warm weather, I wore an overcoat over my uniform and carried the rest of my kit in a carrier bag, not wishing to be mistaken for a real policeman. Outside the station I paused momentarily before presenting myself at the front desk. Waiting to greet me was Sergeant Lewis. I use the word "greet" in its loosest possible sense because the welcome was anything but warm. This came as no surprise to me; I was fully aware that as a brand-new probationary constable, I was the lowest form of animal life in the building, one rung below the prisoners in the cells. I would remain bottom of the food chain until another probationer joined my relief. Ron and Bill had also been posted to Ellesmere Port, but they had been assigned to different shifts, so I was the only rookie on D block. Had

I been the kind of sensitive soul who pondered on these things, I would have no doubt agonised over whether Sgt Lewis genuinely disliked me or whether this was just the way things are in the police service. In any event, I had no intention of dwelling on the issue and was quite prepared to bide my time until I had established some credibility. The Sergeant ushered me into the parade room, the room where each relieving shift gathered to be briefed by their patrol sergeant, and introduced me to my tutor constable, PC Dave Jones. Each new probationer spent his or her first four weeks on division under the watchful eye of a tutor whose job it was to gently ease their charge into the role. Jonesey's welcome was warm and friendly, accompanied by a broad smile and a firm handshake. He looked and sounded the part, and I immediately took to him. Like me, he was in his early twenties but exuded a quiet, assured confidence beyond his years. As an ex-cadet he had joined the regular service at eighteen and a half and now had four years service under his belt. His turnout was immaculate, and it struck me that with the addition of a red sash and pace stick, he could have passed for a drill instructor at Bruche. It was immediately clear to me that I could learn a great deal from Jonesey.

The parade room was dominated by a large, oblong table surrounded by a variety of chairs of varying style, quality, and vintage. At the head of the table were two chairs of rather superior pedigree, almost thronelike with their padded armrests. The walls were adorned with dozens of photographs of suspects and wanted persons, all of whom looked suitably menacing, some of whom looked positively deranged. I stared at one mugshot in particular, convinced that this individual would be of as much interest to the Natural History Museum as the police. Shaven-headed and monobrowed, with wild staring eyes and a protruding jaw, he looked every inch the classic criminal. To add to the overall effect, half of his left ear was missing. In my experience missing ears are something of a lifestyle issue. They are seldom, if ever, accidentally mislaid during the course of some perfectly reasonable and legitimate activity. I and all of my friends and family have two ears, port and starboard, a fact which I pretty much take for granted. Anyway, I suppose with a face like that, crime or horror movies were his only realistic career choices. As I read the handwritten card underneath the snap, two things greatly surprised me. Firstly, he was not called Boris, Krol, Ygor, or indeed anything remotely appropriate. His name was Cyril Rogers. Secondly, the offence for which he was wanted was not mass murder and cannibalism. He was suspected of having obtained a vacuum cleaner by deception. I may be stereotyping here, but I doubt that Cyril was particularly house proud, so why would he want a Hoover? And what half wit could possibly believe him to be a genuine punter? I gave Jonesey a bemused look, to which he smiled and said, "Welcome to Ellesmere Port."

By now the parade room had filled up with my new colleagues, and Jonesey began the round of introductions. Two young PCs, Gareth and Ken, seemed particularly delighted to welcome me. They, like me, were probationers and were, until that day, the bottom of the pecking order. They would now take a step up onto the first rung of the ladder. I expected a range of age groups but was surprised to see that most were in their early to midtwenties. I tried to remember all the names and faces – Ray, Lynn, Stefan, Mark, Chris, Bob, Vicky, Elwyn, Phil. Everyone greeted me with a handshake and a smile, and I felt immediately at home. Ken and Gareth poured mugs of tea from a huge, stainless steel teapot and handed them out to their colleagues, myself included. Gareth patted the teapot and said, "As of today, this is all yours. You have to be in work twenty minutes before everyone else to get the brew sorted. I'll show you where everything is after the parade." In a few months' time I would be able to conduct the ceremony of the teapot and hand over to the newest proby, but for now I was the proud custodian of this gleaming vessel.

Sergeant Lewis walked into the room and sat down in one of the comfy seats at the head of the table, placing a ring binder and a clutch of papers in front of him. With much shuffling of chairs, we took our places around the table. I sat next to Jonesey and placed my pocket notebook on the table in front of me.

"Sit quiet, listen in, and don't speak unless the Sergeant speaks to you. Okay?" said Jonesey.

I nodded obediently whilst writing the time and date in my pocket book.

"Right team, listen in," said the Sergeant, before allocating beats, duties, and refreshment times.

"Jonesey, panda 37/38 with our new probationer, PC Griffin, refs at 1700."

At that moment the parade room door opened, and in walked our boss, Inspector Finnegan.

"Stand up," shouted the Sergeant, and we stood to attention.

"Thank you, Sergeant. Sit down, please," said the Inspector before joining us at the head of the table.

Sergeant Lewis read through the twenty-four-hour arrest

return, the crime register, and the stolen vehicle book. He then summarised the latest report from the local intelligence officer and gave out observations for various wanted persons, including Cyril the Hoover thief.

After ten minutes D Block was on the streets and dealing with incidents, whilst I was given a guided tour of the nick by Jonesey. Gareth was waiting enthusiastically in the kitchen, eager to hand me everything to do with the tea fund. This was clearly a very significant day in Gareth's police career, and the handover complete, he put on his helmet and practically skipped out of the station to patrol the town centre.

Radio room, CID office, custody area, cells, traffic office, and property store were all visited in a whistle stop tour with more introductions and much shaking of hands. After a brief pep talk from Inspector Finnegan and Sgt Lewis, I joined Jonesey for my first operational patrol.

The afternoon shift, 2:00–10:00 p.m., is generally the busiest of the three, and this was no exception. The radio crackled with messages for all available mobiles, and Jonesey and I were dispatched to one incident after another. Troublesome youths and domestic disputes were the order of the day, and I was impressed by the manner in which Jonesey dealt with some very argumentative people without ever appearing to get ruffled.

"Panda 37/38, Are you available for a job at Overpool?"

"37/38, Affirmative. Go ahead with the details – over."

"Report of group of drunken males arguing outside Overpool Road Chip shop – Can you attend? – over."

"En route – over."

Jonesey flicked on the police sign and floored the accelerator. The Vauxhall Viva mustered all of its 1300 cc and took off with much screeching of tyres, belching a plume of black smoke from the exhaust.

Impressive! I thought.

Outside the chip shop a group of a dozen or so young men were jostling and shouting whilst two antagonists squared up for battle. Jonesey pushed his way through the throng, with me in his wake, and approached the drunken pugilists.

"Okay, that's your lot, fellas. On your bikes, the show's over for tonight."

One of the boxers seemed happy to see us, possibly relieved that he was to be spared a beating. He began to back away through the crowd whilst saving face by screaming threats of unspeakable violence at his adversary. The rest, however, were less than pleased at our intervention and the premature end to this free street theatre. They began pushing and shoving us, and it was clear that it only needed one of their number to land a punch before we would be overwhelmed. Jonesey stood firm, arms outstretched with his palms facing towards the crowd.

"Okay, lads, on your way now. You've obviously had a good night, let's not spoil it, eh?" I followed his lead and began ushering the group away from the chip shop with hand gestures and words of encouragement. This was an early lesson in how body language and voice tone can directly affect the outcome of a potentially volatile situation. It was only when they were some distance away that I noticed that one of the two fighters was still standing outside the chip shop. As we made our way to the police car, he followed us in silence, taking up a position by the front nearside headlight.

"Can I help you?" said Jonesey.

"Fuck off!" was the response.

Jonesey walked across to him and looked him in the eye.

"I'll only tell you once, matey, zip it and get on your way, or you're nicked."

"Fuck you!" said the drunk as he launched his fist towards Jonesey's face. In one move Jonesey blocked the punch with his forearm before delivering a resounding slap to the side of the man's head. As our new friend staggered back, stunned by the impact, Jonesey spun him around, threw him across the bonnet of the police car, and handcuffed him behind his back. Jonesey leaned on our prisoner's back and beckoned me over.

"Okay, pal, listen to what this officer's going to tell you," he said. "Go on, Griff, section five public order," he whispered to me.

"You're under arrest for conduct likely to cause a breach of the peace. You're not obliged to say anything, but anything you do say may be given in evidence," I told him.

"Get these cuffs off, and I'll have both of you bastards!" he screamed as we manhandled him into the car.

I lay back and drew heavily on my cigarette. Everyone wants, and to some degree expects, the first time to be memorable. I was no different. This is one of the defining moments in a young man's life, and you only get one shot at it. And now, after much anticipation it had happened. This was a rite of passage which I would remember for the rest of my life.

My first arrest. Yes, I was chuffed, elated – excited even – but to some degree a little disappointed. I felt a bit of a fraud because this was really Jonesey's collar. *Oh well, plenty more where that came from,* I thought.

Jonesey was an inspiration to me. I had no idea what the future held for me and in what direction my chosen career would progress, but I did know one thing for sure. One day I wanted to be as good as Jonesey – that would do for me.

The front garden was littered with rubbish, dog dirt, and discarded pieces of furniture. As I approached the front door of the house, I checked each step carefully, not wishing to step in anything unpleasant. The elderly man who lived here had not been seen for some time, and neighbours had become concerned that something may have happened to him. Even his normally troublesome dog had not disturbed anyone with its incessant barking for some weeks. I pressed my hand against the glass of the front window to shield the reflection of the sun and peered in. The view was obscured by what looked like a black curtain covering the entire window, but on closer examination I saw that this black substance was actually moving. It was millions of bluebottles swarming and wriggling against the glass, desperately trying to get out.

"No way in round the back, Griff. What's the score here?"

Jonesey was making his way across the foetid garden, checking each step exactly as I had done.

I pointed to the window and invited him to look inside, expecting him to exercise some surprise, revulsion, or maybe both. He stepped back, looked at me, and said "Where are your gloves?"

"In my locker," I said. "I'm not cold."

"It's not about keeping warm. It's about keeping clean," he said, removing his truncheon from the long pocket in his trousers.

"What's this for?" he said.

"Self-defence," I said. "But only in an emergency, and blows are to be aimed at the arms and legs, unless you're threatened with a weapon, in which case you can strike the face, head, or groin."

"Very good. Now, forget all that bollocks. This is what a truncheon is for," he said before striking a small pane of glass in the front door. Reaching in through the broken glass, he opened the door. "As for defending yourself or anyone else with a truncheon, forget it. If you get it out, someone's likely to take it off you and shove it where the sun don't shine. Remember that."

The smell inside the hallway of the house was overwhelming – the kind of odour that clings to the face and lips. As Jonesey opened the door to the lounge, we were dive-bombed by escaping bluebottles heading for freedom. The remains of a Border Collie dog lay just inside the doorway, teeth bared in a deathly snarl. Bloated flies flew in and out of its hollowed-out ribcage and performed elaborate aerial displays around the single light bulb hanging in the centre of the room. What remained of the old man who had lived here lay peacefully on a settee, hands gently clasped in front of him. The body was in an advanced state of decomposition and had clearly lain undisturbed for some time. Our normal procedure would have been to strip the body here at the scene and examine it for signs of violence, but clearly that was not going to be an option on this occasion. That examination would take place in the sterile surroundings of the mortuary. The skin of the arms and face varied in colour from a waxy yellow to coal black and didn't really look like human skin at all. One eye was wide open, and his false teeth protruded from the corner of his mouth. Jonesey examined the doors and windows for signs of forced entry but found nothing to indicate that this was a crime scene. We searched for anything of significance – suicide note, medication, signs of a struggle – as I spoke into my radio, requesting that the patrol sergeant and CID be informed. Various documents in the house confirmed the identity of the deceased as Albert Kilbride, aged eighty-three.

Once the police surgeon had attended and declared life extinct, I settled down to await the arrival of the duty undertaker to remove the body. I have never considered myself to be a deep thinker, but there is something about being alone in the company of a dead man which encourages thought about life and death. With the sound of buzzing bluebottles in the background, I looked at this poor man in his ragged clothes and wondered how his journey through life had been. Although I did not know him, I felt sadness that he had died alone in such squalid surroundings. On the sideboard sat a picture of him as a young petty officer in the Royal Navy, his pretty young bride on his arm. Neighbours told us that the man's wife had died some years previously and that he had never really come to terms with his loss, withdrawing to live the life of a hermit. Seeking solace in the bottle, he had become increasingly cantankerous and had long since alienated all well-intentioned helpers. No one visited the house, and there were not believed to be any living relatives, or indeed anyone who might wish to know of his passing. I felt a profound sense of respect for this man whom I had never met in life, and I vowed to afford him whatever dignity I could in death.

Two hours later I was travelling in a hearse with the undertaker to the mortuary at Chester Royal Infirmary. This was the first time I had ever ridden in a hearse, and the thought struck me that at some unknown time in the future, I would make my last trip in one. Maybe I was starting to think too deeply about these things. Jonesey was waiting for me at the hospital, where we stripped the body and bagged up the few items of property found in the trouser pockets. I completed the sudden death form, and we headed back to the nick for a brew and a debrief. Over the course of the coming years I would see many dead bodies and would investigate numerous causes of death, from accidents to suicide and murder, but I would always remember Albert and the few hours we spent together. Rest in peace, my friend.

Foot patrol Town Centre North. With a few genuine arrests under my belt, I was now able to spread my wings and enjoy the freedom of independent patrol. Ellesmere Port in the seventies was a town with two separate and very different identities. South of Westminster Bridge the shopping centre was fairly typical of the era – single storey retail premises and an assortment of office buildings which were home to solicitors, accountants, and the like. With parts of the Marina Walk shopping mall pedestrianised, it was slightly ahead of its time and had quite a modern feel to it. Most of the big retail chains were represented, and the town attracted large crowds of shoppers with its ample parking facilities. The other side of the bridge, however, was a different world entirely. This was the dock area, the birthplace of the original town and the reason for its very existence. In the late eighteenth century, the Ellesmere Canal connected the town of Ellesmere in Shropshire with the sea, and a port developed near to the village of Netherpool. As the population of the village grew, it became known as the Port of Ellesmere, changing its name to Ellesmere Port in the early nineteenth century. By the mid-twentieth century, thanks to the opening of the Manchester Ship Canal in 1894, the town was booming, and the docks were handling huge numbers of ships from all over the world. Like dock areas the world over, a lively and colourful community sprang up around the dockside with pubs, shops, and various entrepreneurs eager to separate sailors from their hard-earned cash. By the late seventies the gradual decline of the docks had begun, but this was still a wild and wonderful world, somewhat reminiscent of the Popeye cartoons of my youth. It had an exotic feel to it with its dingy, smoky pubs frequented by seamen from Scandinavia, Russia, and the Far East. The Norwegians in particular were regular visitors: big, tough men with elaborate tattoos and huge hands; Smiling, gregarious men who consumed spectacular amounts of alcohol before availing themselves of the services of the many working girls who earned a crust in this murky parallel universe.

Church Parade was a row of a dozen or so small shops a little way back from the docks. At night this was a desolate and depressing place. The shop fronts disappeared behind steel shutters, each scrawled with graffiti. The pedestrianised walkway was strewn with fish and chip papers, dog dirt, and invariably a used condom or two. Crushed beer cans and a dirty syringe lay outside the hairdressers shop as I walked past, reading some of the new graffiti. A small triangular sticker on one of the steel shutters announced "Jesus Saves", to which some wag had added "But Keegan Scores off the Rebound". An old joke, I know, but it made me smile that rainy, cold night as I meandered around that godforsaken place. Suddenly I heard the sound of drunken singing and saw three clearly inebriated men round the corner and walk towards me. "Kalyinka, Kalyinka, Kalyinka Malya," or something similar was the refrain. I recognised this as a Russian song but had no idea what the words meant. The three men approached me, and one of their number offered his outstretched hand. "Hello, my friend. You drink with me?" he said before offering me a half empty bottle of clear liquid. I shook his hand and explained that I wasn't allowed to drink on duty. He regarded me in a bemused way, looked at the bottle, and took a large swig before again offering it to me. I got the impression that he was demonstrating that the drink wasn't poisoned.

My reluctance to imbibe with my new friends was not so much in deference to police regulations; it was more to do with the fact that I wasn't a big fan of 100 proof Russian vodka, particularly when served at room temperature and liberally laced with saliva. In the interests of international relations, however, I took the bottle from him and pressed it against my closed lips. Remember that the Cold War was at its height at this time, and I had no wish to spark a nuclear conflagration.

"Naztrovya!" they shouted in unison as I pretended to drink this Sputnik fuel.

"Naztrovya," I said as I handed back the bottle.

"We like make dance with lady. You know where we go?" said the spokesman.

I knew exactly where they go. Chez Henry's International Club. That's where they go.

"Follow me," I said, and we set off on the short walk to the leading night spot that side of Westminster Bridge. They launched into another chorus of Kalyinka, and in a spirit of "What the hell" I joined in, to their delight and amusement.

Chez Henry's was a small night club at the far end of Church Parade. It was actually a converted shop unit with the plate glass windows painted black and was on the small side. An estate agent would probably describe it as compact, bijoux, and atmospheric; anyone else would call it a shithole. When I first saw the place, I assumed its name was pronounced "Shay OnREE" like the French which I remembered from my school days. But no, this was Ellesmere Port, and it was pronounced Chez Enreez, just like it said over the door. Another sign over the door proudly boasted "London – Paris – Milan" so it would appear that this was just one of four similar establishments across Europe. I wondered if the London club had a sign saying "Paris – Milan – Ellesmere Port". Probably not.

Formal introductions were made during the short walk, and Oleg, Vladimir, and Leonid proved to be affable companions. I introduced myself as Griff, but the pronunciation proved impossible for three drunken Russians. After numerous failed attempts, ranging from "Khareef" to "Guruf", they reverted to calling me "Meester".

As introductions to the bourgeois decadence of the West go, I suspect that Chez Henry's was something of a disappointment. I opened the front door and gestured for my friends to enter, to which they seemed surprisingly reluctant. A cloud of cigarette smoke hung over the small dance floor as a mass of bodies gyrated to the strains of "Hotel California" by the Eagles. Seated at a table just inside the front door was Martha, who beckoned the three sailors over and opened a big red book. Martha was a lady of indeterminate age and dubious fashion sense. Her arms were adorned with flamboyant and very artistic tattoos which had undoubtedly cost her a considerable amount of money. Such extravagance had clearly left little in the kitty for dental care and her teeth were a truly shocking spectacle. Ranging in colour from yellow through beige to brown, they looked like rows of long neglected headstones.

"This is a private club, but for thirty-five pence you can become a member," she said.

"Yes, very good. We like," said Oleg as he began filling in details in the membership book.

"Thirty-five pence?" I said to Martha as Vladimir added his name and address in his best Cyrillic Script.

"To keep the riffraff out," said Martha.

A casual glance around the room suggested that the policy wasn't working.

"See you, fellas," I said as I headed out into the rain.

"Thank you, Meester – Daz Vadanya," shouted Oleg.

Jonesey's panda car screeched to a halt outside The Welcome chip shop, and I jumped in the passenger seat.

"Auto alarm at Motorfactors on the Thornton Estate Griff. It's been done twice in the last month – could be game on," he said as we sped through the traffic lights and over the bridge. When we were within a few hundred yards of the premises, Jonesey turned off the lights and slowed down, stopping some way short of the gates. We both sprinted towards the small industrial unit, which was surrounded by a ten-foot-high wire mesh security fence, and I threw myself at the gate. Clinging on with my fingertips, I climbed to the top of the structure before executing an impressive commando roll, ready to begin my descent down the other side. I was, however, stopped in my tracks when I felt the gate begin to move. I looked down to see Jonesey opening it and walking in. He glanced up at me, closed the gate, and walked towards the door of the premises. In my mind's eye I could see Lindop pointing up at me atop the steel gate, legs akimbo. I could almost hear him saying, "There you are – I told you he was an imbecile."

There have no doubt been occasions in my life when I have made a bigger fool of myself, but I am hard pressed to think of one. The activation was a false alarm, and on the journey back to the nick the gate incident was not mentioned. Jonesey was astute enough to understand my embarrassment, and no words were necessary. I was concerned that he would reveal to everyone back at the station what a complete tosser I was, but I need not have worried – he told no one.

Town Centre North was the least popular foot beat, but I grew to like this place. As the weeks and months passed it became my world. I was growing in confidence and getting to know many of the characters who contributed to this rich tapestry, in particular the many prostitutes who plied their ancient trade around the dockside pubs. Under English law it has never been an offence to give or receive sexual favours for payment, so the working girls made no secret of their activities. There are, however, many offences connected with the manner in which these services are provided, and all of the girls were well versed in the legislation. Soliciting for prostitution, operating a brothel, importuning, and living off immoral earnings were all specifically outlawed, but in this twilight world around the docks, it was a case of live and let live. The sailors who came ashore wanted alcohol, food, and sex in that order, and the girls were as much a part of the scene as were the pubs, clubs, and fast food joints.

Shirley was old school, a professional who had strong views about some of the younger girls attracted to the streets by the prospect of easy money.

"It's not like the old days, Griff," she said to me as we strolled past the Grosvenor Pub on Dock Street. "These youngsters take risks. They work alone, they'll go with anybody, and they'll do anything. It's all drugs now, that's what's made the difference. You've got to keep your dignity in this game. If you do that, then the punters will respect you and you won't come to any harm."

Shirley was in semiretirement but retained a regular and loyal clientele among some of the sailors who were frequent visitors. She also performed the roles of shop steward, health visitor, and social worker for the other girls who worked this patch. She had a heart of gold and had clearly kept her dignity. I respected her.

We said our goodbyes outside the Grosvenor, and Shirley headed off to meet a punter.

"Be careful, Shirl," I shouted as she wandered off into the night. She turned around, winked, and blew me a kiss. At that point a Vauxhall Viva caught my attention as it turned onto the pub car park. I noticed that the offside quarter light window was smashed and there were four young men aboard. I considered it worth a check and made my way towards it, arriving just as the four men were heading into the pub.

"Can I have a word?" I shouted to the man who had got out of the driver's seat.

"What?" he said.

"Is this your car?" I said.

"Don't know anything about any car, mate"

He was about to walk on as I put my hand on his shoulder and said, "I'm arresting you on suspicion of theft of this vehicle."

He immediately aimed a punch at my face, making a glancing contact under my left eye and sending my helmet skidding across the car park. The three other men had stopped in the doorway of the pub and were now making their way towards me. Realising that I was in trouble, I took a step back and shouted into my radio.

"Assistance required – Grosvenor Pub – Dock Street," I yelled, hoping that the message had been received and understood back at the nick. I then grabbed my assailant in a kind of bear hug, pinning his arms to his side. As we both fell backwards against a small wall, his three pals began to rain down kicks and punches, the majority of which landed on my prisoner. Some of the blows, however, did find their intended target, and I took a full blooded kick to the side of my ribs. After hearing my assistance call being given out over the radio, I was determined to hang on to my prisoner, using him as a human shield until the cavalry arrived. It was probably no more than two minutes before I heard the sound of screeching tyres and saw the blue lights of two patrol cars, but it seemed like forever. The three men ran off towards the docks, and my human body armour suddenly became all smiles and bonhomie.

"Sorry mate, no problems, eh," he said, as I dragged him to his feet and threw him against a parked car. Pumped up with adrenaline and testosterone, I made a fist with my favoured right hand and grabbed him tightly around the throat with my left. I was sorely tempted to land a punch on the corner of his jaw, standing for some seconds considering it. There was genuine terror in his eyes, and I'm ashamed to say that I was pleased to see his fear. Maybe there's a bully in all of us.

"Okay, Griff," said Sgt Lewis. "Stick him in here." He opened the police car door.

I cautioned and cuffed my prisoner and shoved him into the back seat, slamming the door as hard as I could to release the pent up aggression.

"You all right?" said the Sergeant.

"A few bruises but I'll live, Sarge," I replied. "I'm just glad you heard the assistance call. Thanks."

"Actually we didn't hear anything; you know what reception is like down here. We got an anonymous phone call from a woman who saw you in trouble," he said.

I looked across the road to see Shirley standing by a telephone kiosk. I gave her a wave and a smile. "Be careful, Griff!" she shouted before heading off back to work.

Prostitutes, like police officers, inhabit a murky and often dangerous world where violence is a constant threat. Over the years many working girls have become murder victims, and I have heard ill informed people comment that they have

69

in some way deserved their fate. Whenever I hear people say these things, it makes me very angry.

It was the early hours of a bitterly cold January morning as Ken and I pulled out of the police station yard and headed out to complete the last few hours of the night shift. Ken had only recently completed his driving course and was enjoying the extra freedom which came with mobile patrol. The panda beats were much sought after and jealously guarded by the more senior members of D Block, so new drivers had to wait their turn before being given the keys to one of the pale blue and white Vauxhall Vivas. Tonight was Ken's chance to spread his wings, and he was keen to get amongst the action. By 3:00 a.m., however, there was little action to be had as we cruised around the town. As we pulled up at a set of traffic lights, I decided, for no particular reason, to run a check on the car in front of us.

"37/38 – PNC vehicle check, please."

37/38 – Go ahead with your details."

"Austin 1300 in brown, registered number Whisky November Oscar Nine Three Zero Foxtrot."

"Vehicle reported stolen 11:00 p.m., 3 January."

"37/38 – We're behind vehicle now in Whitby Road. Two males aboard. Attempting stop outside Viscount public house. Stand by."

The driver had noticed our interest, and the car took off with a screeching of tyres. As Ken set off in pursuit, I gave a running commentary over the radio. The Austin went through red lights and across give way junctions without pause, clearly oblivious to the dangers to themselves or others. Ken drew on all the skills taught during his four-week driving course to keep up with our quarry without being reckless. The car went onto two wheels as it lurched to its left, clipping a parked van in the process before turning into Mill Lane. The route it had taken took it to Rivacre Valley, which Ken and I knew to be a dead end. The concrete bollards at its far end would prove more than a match for a clapped out Austin 1300, and I undid my seat belt in readiness for the inevitable.

As the bollards came into view, the red brake lights came on, and the stolen car began to skid sideways as both doors opened simultaneously. As the police car shuddered to a halt, I leapt out and went in pursuit of the front seat passenger. Rivacre Brook is usually a fairly benign waterway, little more than a stream, but after a week of torrential winter rain it had become a raging torrent. It had risen several feet higher than normal up its grassy banks, its muddy waters swirling and crashing into tree stumps as it raced angrily downstream. My prey was about twenty yards ahead of me, sprinting along the river bank and checking over his shoulder every few steps. Suddenly and without warning, he leapt into the raging water and began wading across to the other bank. He was up to his neck in the filthy water but was making good progress and looking confident. Without thought I too leapt into the brook, immediately losing my footing and disappearing under the surface. I was swept downstream, inhaling a lungful of water in the process, and I was now in severe difficulty. Unable to get a foothold, I was being carried away by the sheer power of the water and was genuinely concerned that I would drown. Having given up any hope of being able to stand up, I grabbed an overhanging branch and was able to steady myself. I then began pulling myself in towards dry land as I saw my prisoner scrambling out and crawling on all fours up the muddy bank. Having pulled myself clear of the water, I began to crawl up the bank, more determined than ever to make the arrest. There then followed what must have been the slowest chase in history as he and I crawled on our hands and knees up a forty-five-degree muddy embankment. I had considered myself to be quite fit, but by now my heart felt as though it was about to burst as I got to my feet and staggered after my car thief. He disappeared down an alleyway between some houses, and I began to fear that my swimming had been in vain. Oh well, at least Sgt Storr would have been impressed. Guessing that he was as exhausted as I was, I thought he was more likely to hide than to continue running, so I stopped and listened. To amplify any sound in the night air, I opened my mouth wide and held my breath. Just a few feet away from me I could hear the sound of heavy breathing. I walked towards the sound whilst pretending to speak into my radio, saying I had lost the offender and was heading back to the car. Behind a bush lay my prize, and I threw myself on top of him, determined that he would not escape. "You're locked up for theft of that car," I shouted as I gripped him in a headlock.

"I'm, knackered," he said.

"Me too, mate," I replied.

I pulled him to his feet, and we stood looking at each other. I reached out to put my handcuffs on him, and he offered me his hand to shake. Having placed the cuff around his wrist I accepted his offer of a handshake, and we both began to laugh out loud.

"I didn't think you'd come after me in the water," he said.

"D'you realise we both could have died? Anyway, you're

not obliged to say anything unless you wish to do so, but anything you say may be given in evidence," I said.

"Could do with a brew," he replied.

Back at the nick Sgt Lewis handed me one of the white paper suits which were issued to prisoners when their clothes were seized for forensic examination and suggested that I get changed and go home. I was more than happy to accept his offer of an early finish, but not before I had shared a cup of tea with my prisoner in his cell.

Leslie Guntripp was a solitary character who lived an obsessively private life in his isolated cottage in the countryside outside Winsford. No one knew anything of his daily routine, and aside from the postman, no one ever went near his home. He was not in the habit of entertaining guests, but on a cold February evening all those years ago there had clearly been at least one visitor to that remote house. That much was certain because in the living room of his house, Mr Guntripp had been murdered.

I was one of a team of uniformed officers brought in to conduct house-to-house inquiries in the surrounding area and was relishing the opportunity to become involved in a major enquiry. Even the victim's name had a slightly Agatha Christie quality about it. That first morning we were gathered together in a school hall to be briefed by the CID team leading the hunt for Mr Guntripp's killer. I had been collected from Ellesmere Port Police Station in a personnel carrier and had struck up a friendship with PC Ray Davenport during the journey to Winsford. Ray was based at Chester and was a few years my senior, so I was grateful for his experience and advice about what

73

lay ahead. Unlike the mysteries of popular fiction, real murders are not solved by solitary detectives using brilliant powers of deduction. A successful conclusion is the result of thousands of hours of painstaking investigation by teams of detectives assisted by uniformed staff, scene of crime officers, civilian administrators, and many other back-room staff. The murder of Mr Guntripp would prove particularly challenging because it lacked virtually all of the elements required to build up a profile of his killer or killers. There were no suspects, no apparent motive, no witnesses, and very little forensic evidence in these days before the development of DNA analysis. There was no murder weapon left at the scene, although the head injuries suggested some type of blunt instrument.

After the briefing we were split into teams off six, each led by a sergeant. I was pleased to be teamed up with Ray. The team issued us folders containing hundreds of questionnaire pro formas, and we were dropped off at various locations to knock on doors and complete a form for every occupant. The aim was, if necessary, to interview every single resident of Winsford, a town of some fifty-five thousand people at the time. I soon realised that this task was likely to be light on excitement and felt somewhat deflated. Ray noted my mood and offered some sound advice.

"Chin up, mate," he said. "You may touch lucky and end up locking up the killer. Not bad for a proby, eh?"

"Unlikely," I said.

"Anyway, house to house is what you make of it," said Ray. "Always remember you may just pick up that vital piece of the jigsaw. Don't just fill in the form. Ask who they think could have done something like this. If he's local someone will know, or guess, who he is. But they won't tell you unless you ask. If you think they're lying about something, then ask them questions that you know they will answer truthfully, like their grandparents names or what football team they support – anything at all. Then compare how they react when telling the truth to how they look when you think they're lying. You know, fidgeting, scratching, looking away – that kind of thing. Remember, you're not just filling in forms. You're trying to detect a murder, so stay switched on and be professional. Apart from anything else, it makes the time go quicker, believe me."

I took Ray's advice and stayed switched on and professional throughout the three weeks that I worked on the enquiry. I learned a tremendous amount about asking questions and listening to answers and soon discovered that there was more to this than met the eye.

Unfortunately neither I nor any other member of the team picked up the vital piece of the jigsaw, and Mr Guntripp's killer was never identified. The fact that this person could still be alive and walking the streets today does concern me, but it in no way detracts from the advice given to me by Ray. Over the years I would remember his wise words, often quoting them to others and always claiming them as my own.

During those few weeks Ray and I became good mates, travelling to and from work together in my car. He was my friend and mentor, and from our conversations I learned lessons which helped shape the way I thought and behaved as I progressed through my career. I expected that we would remain close throughout our service, so it was with some sadness that I learned of his intention to leave Cheshire Police and transfer to Merseyside. Just a few months later he had gone, moving to Merseyside Police's Task Force. Friendships in the police tend to be intense but often transient and temporary. Ray had moved on, and I suspected that that was the last I would ever hear of him. I was wrong.

Neston Police Station had been built in 1936, and had changed little during the ensuing forty or so years. It was an impressive edifice, designed and constructed during a period when public buildings were expected to make a bold statement. To the front of it was a large lawn dominated by an octagonal concrete feature, rather like a bandstand but without the roof. In the centre of that was the flag pole, from which the Union Flag flew proudly every day of the year. The police station itself occupied the ground floor whilst the first floor housed two magnificent magistrates courts, the opulence of which was staggering. Court number one was the flagship, with its oak panels and green leather upholstered seating. Entry to the prisoner's dock was gained via a marble stair case which led directly to the cells below. Detainees appearing at this court were afforded the full majesty of the law with none of the undignified shuffling through the public area that was customary elsewhere. They appeared as if by magic in the dock, rather like the famous organist at Blackpool's Tower Ballroom. For a prisoner enjoying this rather theatrical entrance for the first time, it must have been a memorable if sobering experience. As a newly qualified police driver, there was now more to my world than meandering around town centre north and wondering what to do with the drunken sailor. Panda beat 39/40 covered Neston, Parkgate, Willaston, and Burton and was an altogether different experience to the grimy docklands of Ellesmere Port.

The sun shone down from a cloudless azure sky as I parked the panda car in front of the main entrance of the nick and headed inside for my refreshment break. It had been unusually quiet that day, and I felt relaxed and contented as I settled down to my sandwiches in the rest room. I suspect that the only thing in that room which had not been included in the original manifest of 1936 was the small portable TV that sat on the solid wooden table where I unwrapped my lunch. I switched the TV on to see that the peace and tranquillity which I was enjoying did not prevail twenty-five miles away across the River Mersey. On the screen I saw lines of police officers crouched behind riot shields as hordes of youths and men bombarded them with bricks and petrol bombs. The name "Toxteth" was rapidly becoming etched in the public psyche as this desolate area on the edge of Liverpool, gaining worldwide notoriety. Many of our colleagues had already been injured, some seriously, and there was real concern that the rule of the mob could prevail.

As I watched the newsreel footage, PC Phil Kaye came into the room. "Have you heard the news?" he said.

"Shush," I said. "I'm watching it now."

"No," said Phil, "not that. I mean about the bobby murdered last night. He was trying to arrest some car thieves. Don't know the details, but they killed him."

"Who?" I said.

"I don't know the lad personally. Someone called Ray Davenport."

Clearly this could not be true. There must be some mistake. Ray dead? No way.

There was no mistake. Ray had been questioning the driver of a car when he discovered that the vehicle was stolen. He leaned in to grab the ignition keys, and the driver drove off, with Ray hanging out of the side window. The driver deliberately drove into a concrete bus shelter to get him off the car, causing massive internal injuries from which he soon died. Three men were arrested at the scene.

I felt a range of emotions as I sat in front of the TV trying to come to terms with what had happened – shock, anger, sorrow, and a sense of utter disbelief.

The riots which had begun in Toxteth soon spread to other parts of the country, and public disorder became the number one news item throughout that long, hot summer. Against that backdrop Ray's death didn't make the national news.

That upset me. It still does.

"Right, gentlemen. Busy minute. Starting with a loaded, holstered weapon, on the whistle sprint to your target and then back to the barricade. Standing at the barricade, body shot left, body shot right. Kneeling position, body shot left, body shot right. Prone position, body shot left, body shot right. Reload with six rounds in the prone and then repeat the shoot. Back to the kneel, and reload with four rounds. Stand clear of the barricade – headshot right, headshot left. Final two rounds – body shot left, body shot right. Any questions?" Sergeant Mick Farr allowed a momentary pause before the shrill screech of the whistle pierced the air. I set off as fast as my legs would carry me, knowing that a swift return to the start point was required to allow as much time as possible for good, well-aimed shots.

The Smith and Wesson .38 Special revolver was the standard police hand gun at the time, and to remain on the list of authorised firearms officers it was necessary to requalify on the ranges at regular intervals. The requal shoot involved firing fifty rounds at a variety of targets under varying conditions, and a score of 70 per cent was required, although anything less than 80 per cent was frowned upon. This was easier said than done because all the shooting was done under stressful conditions and against the clock. Confidence and good weapon handling skills were as important as accuracy, as was a fair degree of physical fitness. Those who failed to reach the pass mark were given one more opportunity. Anyone failing at the second attempt was invited back in a week's time and given one practice run and then a third and final opportunity to achieve the required 70 per cent. All of this made for a nerve-racking experience because no one wanted to face the humiliation of losing their authority. The .38 Special is a good and reliable handgun, but between ten and thirty meters it is surprisingly easy to miss a man-sized target, particularly when out of breath.

Having completed the shoot with a few seconds to spare, I held up my revolver for one of the instructors to check that the chamber was empty, and then I reholstered it and stood facing the targets. Sgt Farr and the two PC instructors approached the targets to check our scores, patching up the bullet holes with small paper stickers as they counted up the number of hits.

"Mr Pearson – All on. Mr Macey – All on. Mr Griffin – fourteen," shouted the Sergeant. The busy minute was never my best event, but this time I was confident that I had got all my rounds on target and in the required order. Both of my headshots, however, had missed. To be fair, one had parted the bad guy's hair and on another day may have been counted as a hit. The other had by all accounts flown some twenty feet above my target, sending up a plume of sand from the butts and seriously frightening some nearby pigeons. Not good. Flyaway rounds are one of the cardinal sins of police shooting, and for very good reason: on the streets a flyer could hit an innocent member of the public. Unlike military shooting, where it is often a good and valid tactic to loose off a quick volley of shots in the general direction of your target, every police bullet must be accounted for. Sgt Farr approached me with a look of concern and held out his hand for my weapon. Having removed it from its leather holster, I opened the chamber to demonstrate that it was unloaded and handed it to him.

"You're still snatching that trigger, Griff," he said. "Watch me. Punch it out in front of you, get a good sight picture, lock the right elbow, and squeeeeeze. Okay?"

"Got it, Sarge," I said as he handed my revolver back to me.

"You say that every time. Load with six rounds and give me six headshots from ten meters in your own time."

Six headshots. Six hits.

"Easy when there's no pressure, isn't it?" said the Sergeant. "Problem is when you do it for real, you will be under pressure."

Shooting a suspect in the head may sound extreme, but it was a skill we had to practice due to the ready availability of body armour. Irish Republican terrorism was at its height at the time, and the terrorists routinely wore Kevlar body armour under their shirts. Some professional armed robbers were also beginning to wear body armour, so the ability to put a round into a suspect's head was crucial. Unlike the gunslingers of the Wild West we did not attempt to disarm the bad guys with arm and leg shots. Police will only open fire when there is an immediate and deadly threat, and under those circumstances the aim is to neutralise that threat in short order. A well-executed headshot does just that. My headshots that day were clearly cause for concern – one hairdressing round and one pigeon scarer – and not for the first time I was going to have to buck my ideas up.

My final score for the hand gun that day came out at 74 per cent. Enough to requalify but clearly not enough to satisfy Sgt Farr, who shook his head as he filled in the range report on his clipboard. Next up was the Remington pump action shotgun, a crude weapon with one hell of a recoil that left the shoulder black and blue after just a few rounds had been fired off. The pressure, however, was off by this time because we had all requalified with the revolver, and that was what counted. Despite this, I was not happy with my performance. It seemed that a pattern of mediocrity was becoming the common thread running through my career. I was achieving just enough to get by but never really excelling at anything. I wanted to be good, not just good enough. Maybe the police service wasn't for me after all; maybe I had made a bad choice. Applying for the police was something which I had done on a whim; it had never been a childhood ambition of mine. As a boy I had always been something of a dreamer, and my dream had been to join the French Foreign Legion. As all good Englishmen should, I had read Wren's *Beau Geste* and had been captivated by the story. The image of the Tricoleur fluttering above Fort Zinderneuf as the Legionnaires looked out across the shimmering sands of the Sahara had made a lasting impression on me. I spent countless hours at the library reading books on the history and traditions of the Legion and even memorised the words to "Le Boudin", the marching song of this famous corps. I could sing it for you now. If you want.

For a whole variety of reasons I had not followed my dream, and as I drove home from the ranges that day, the thought struck me that maybe I should have. I still had the address of the recruiting office at Fort de Nogent in Paris, so maybe it wasn't too late. On the other hand, if I can't score a headshot with a revolver, am I likely to be any more effective at leading a bayonet charge across the shifting sands of the desert? Possibly not. By the time I got home, I had decided to stay with Cheshire Police and put all thoughts of La Legion Etrangere behind me. For now.

CHAPTER 4

Criminal Investigation Department

For a country where the game of baseball is very much a minority interest, it always struck me as rather odd that the home of every criminal in the land contains at least one baseball bat. What is even more strange is that at none of these homes did I ever come across a ball. Also, aside from the occasional cap, I have never found any of the other paraphernalia traditionally associated with the sport. Pitcher's gloves, spiked shoes, numbered shirts, and those rather natty skintight pants are never anywhere to be seen. It all tends to suggest that when these aficionados get together to enjoy a game, things must fall terribly flat. Having stood around in a local park for hours on end swinging the bat at thin air, is it any wonder that frustration sets in and the players resort to clubbing each other over the head? I strongly suspect that this is exactly what had happened that Autumn afternoon in Whitby Park, when one of our local drug dealers had sustained some very impressive head wounds at the hands of Cyril Rogers, the one-eared Hoover thief. The motive was unclear, and it is not my place to be judgemental. Maybe Cyril was acting as some kind of vigilante filled with righteous rage at the open sale of narcotics on the streets of his hometown. More likely, however, as a regular customer of this dealer, there had been a quality of service issue which Cyril had resolved in his own unique way. Whilst some would deal with such a customer complaint by instructing a solicitor, Cyril preferred a more direct approach. He had been arrested by the CID whilst drinking in a pub near to the scene, and I was on my way to search his house for the weapon or anything else of evidential value. Experience told me that the bat would be somewhere just inside the front door, close to hand and ready to greet any unexpected and unwelcome visitors, be they police officers, double glazing salesmen, or those charming young American boys from the Church of the Latter Day Saints. Using Cyril's Yale key, I opened the front door, and voila: one baseball bat leaning against the electricity cupboard, complete with bloodstains, hair, and bits of skin – perfect. I placed the bat in an evidence bag and generally rummaged around the place for as long as I could tolerate the smell, which reminded me of the elephant house at Chester Zoo. Back at the nick I booked my exhibit into the property system and added it to our ever growing collection of baseball bats.

Personally, I find this British obsession with all things American rather depressing. Here in England we have the perfect piece of sporting equipment which can double as an offensive weapon: the cricket bat. Wouldn't it be far nicer to see our local villains taking the field armed with this iconic and quintessentially English item? Better still if they were fully kitted out in whites and Panama hat. How refreshing it would be to hear the click of willow on skull, a gentle ripple of polite applause, and an appreciative chorus of "Well played, Sir!"

Coincidentally, a game of cricket was in full swing in the CID office as I walked in with the paperwork for the Rogers job. Detective Sergeant Martin Goulding was at the crease, bat in hand and ready to receive a ball from DC Howard Davison. Howard was rubbing the battered tennis ball vigorously against his upper thigh as the fielders positioned themselves at strategic points around the office. Now, you may think it strange that detectives play cricket in the office, but I was not in the least surprised by the scene which greeted me that day. I had previously interrupted games of football, rugby, and basketball, as well as a bizarre pastime known as Indian Leg Wrestling. Similar to arm wrestling, but using the legs, this was an activity completely new and unknown to me. I asked numerous Indian waiters if they were familiar with the sport, but none of them had ever heard of it. Maybe its origins lie in North America, but I suspect it was invented and developed in Ellesmere Port CID office.

That day, however, cricket was the sport of choice, and Martin had a look of grim determination on his face as he steadied himself for the delivery. The somewhat cramped conditions meant that the bowler's run up was very limited, but this did not prevent Howard launching a fierce ball straight at Martin's midriff, bodyline style. Martin swung the bat and made glancing contact, first with the ball and then with some tea cups on the desk behind him. The ball flew across the office and out of an open window; the cups fell to the floor and shattered like fragmentation grenades.

"Time for lunch, gentlemen," said Martin, placing the bat under his arm and walking towards his desk.

"Mission accomplished," I said as I handed him a written statement and an exhibit label. "It's in the property store."

"Thanks, Griff. Are you able to do the interview? We've got a job on this afternoon." said Martin.

"You're going to have to pack it in, Martin. The Super's fuming," someone said from behind me.

I turned around to see Ruth, the Superintendent's secretary, standing at the office door with a very serious look on her face. The Divisional Commander's office was directly below, and he was apparently furious about the noise generated by the high jinks above.

"What do you mean?" said Martin.

"I mean you lot playing cricket," said Ruth.

"Cricket? What are you talking about?" said Martin, bat tucked firmly under his arm.

"You're like kids," said Ruth. "Just pack it in, okay?"

"I'm afraid that's not possible," said Martin.

"Not possible? What do mean?" said Ruth in astonishment.

"Well, it's the final day of the third test, and we only need four more runs for a draw," said Martin.

I loved the lunacy of the CID office and it was probably that more than anything else which convinced me that I wanted to be a detective. After six months on attachment as a CID aide and having successfully navigated the three-week course and written examination, I was placed on the list for appointment as a detective as and when a vacancy arose. Meanwhile, it was back to uniformed duties as a panda car driver. As an authorised firearms officer, I was regularly called away for training, requalification, and operations, so there was always plenty going on and life was good. So good in fact that I had entirely given up on any ideas of joining the Legion. Well, almost entirely.

When I was offered the opportunity of a six-month secondment to the Force Burglary Squad, I jumped at the chance, seeing it as good preparation for a CID post. The squad was a covert team that targeted known burglars, carrying out surveillance and gathering evidence which was then handed over to local CID officers, who made the arrests. We were trained in mobile surveillance using high-powered vehicles fitted with covert car-to-car radio. We also received training in following suspects on foot, and I found the whole thing exciting and immensely enjoyable. The team was a mix of people – some like me waiting to be appointed to CID duties, others budding traffic cops keen to hone their driving skills in this unique, sneaky beaky environment. We were very ably led by DS Sheila Lloyd, a seasoned detective who could smell a thief at five hundred yards on a clear day.

It was a miserable, grey day as we checked our vehicles in the yard of Warrington Police Station. I was teamed up with Owen, who had recently passed his advanced driving course and was awaiting a posting to the Regional Crime Squad. We headed out of the station yard to our appointed static observation point where we parked up to await developments. On my clipboard I had a list of vehicles known to be used by local criminals, and it wasn't long before we spotted one of them pull up outside a betting shop. Two young men got out and entered the bookies.

I pressed the radio transmit button under my seat and spoke into the covert microphone hidden behind the sun visor.

"Griff to convoy. Target vehicle red Ford Cortina, Uniform Yankee Bravo Five Two Seven Golf, parked outside William

Hill betting shop in Bellefield Avenue. Two male occupants in shop. Stand by."

The convoy consisted of three other cars and a motorcycle and was ready nearby to pick up the follow when the suspect vehicle was on the move.

"Griff to convoy, two white males back in vehicle, stand by."

"Griff with the eyeball, target off, off, off. Bellefield Avenue towards town centre. Speed three five, two vehicle cover at forty meters. Convoy check."

"Leo, back up in your mirror."

"Road Runner number three."

"Macker number four, Griff."

"Porky, tail end Charlie."

All this chat was standard surveillance jargon, and the same terminology was used by police officers across the UK. Whilst it may sound strange, the choice of words was designed to avoid any possibility of confusion in what could be a fast moving and complex environment. The word "eyeball", for instance, has a very specific meaning and indicates direct, positive visual contact with the target. Also, when radio transmission may be crackly, it is a word which can be clearly heard and understood. Nicknames were used rather than call signs, and the convoy check indicated that the team was in place and in the correct order for a covert follow. I was the lead, or eyeball car followed by the second, or backup car. The motorcycle was in third spot, another car at four, and the last car was tail end Charlie. Other random vehicles were deliberately allowed to separate the team vehicles so as not to alert the suspects, and the eyeball car would never, ever be directly behind the target vehicle. After a number of turns or deviations, the eyeball car would allow the backup car to take over, or pick up eyeball, and the eyeball car would move to tail end Charlie. All of this meant that the suspects would never notice that they were being followed, and we had practised the technique to perfection.

After an hour or so tailing our Cortina without incident, Sgt Lloyd decided to call off the follow and arrange for a marked car to stopcheck it. Just as we were about to abort, however, the Cortina took off at high speed, and Owen couldn't resist giving chase. This was a cardinal sin because it was not our job to carry out a pursuit, and Sgt Lloyd was furious. Our cover was blown, we were chasing a suspect vehicle at high speed in an unmarked car, we were in the shit – and we were having the time of our lives. To make matters worse, the rest of the team had joined in as we headed out of town and out onto the open road. Sgt Lloyd was screaming down the radio telling us to abort, but Owen was like the master of the Cheshire Hunt, and the fox was in sight. Tally Ho!

We chased the car into countryside north of Warrington and had no idea where we were. Behind us I could see road runner (the motorbike) and Leo, but there was no sign of the other two cars. I later found out that in their enthusiasm to join in the fun, they had crashed into each other. We followed the Cortina off road onto some farm land and were making ground on it when it did a handbrake turn and headed directly at us. Owen lurched to our left before flooring the accelerator and driving straight at the offside of the suspect's car.

"Permission to ram, Admiral?" he said as we hurtled towards our target.

"Carry on, Captain," I replied, not at all certain of the legality of my decision.

We hit the car broadside with a satisfying thrump, and the passenger flew out of the nearside door like a cork being fired from a bottle of vintage Champagne. Owen took off like a greyhound and rugby tackled him some fifty or so meters away. I leapt onto the bonnet of our ruined car, leaned through the smashed side window of the Cortina, and grabbed the driver by the throat, squeezing until his face turned a rather alarming shade of purple. Within seconds a marked traffic car was on the scene, and we placed our prisoners in the back of it. Having organised a tow vehicle to recover the two wrecked cars, Owen and I hitched a lift with the traffic car back to Warrington Police Station.

We were both on a high having had a thoroughly enjoyable afternoon, and it wasn't until we got closer to the nick that I began to have some concerns about what reception awaited us there. We had gone against force policy by becoming involved in a pursuit in an unmarked car. We had disobeyed a lawful order to abort the chase. We had driven off-road in contravention of everything we had been taught during our driving courses. We had completely blown the cover of the covert vehicle fleet. We had deliberately rammed a vehicle, written off a police car, and been indirectly responsible for damage to two more. I had attempted to choke one of the suspects, who was already talking of making an official complaint, and we weren't entirely sure what offence, if any, they had committed. Hmm. Where did I put that bit of paper with the address of the Foreign Legion Recruiting Office?

Conceived during the late 1800s when Britain was at the height of its colonial power, Warrington Police Station sits majestically on the edge of the town centre, next to Bank Quay Railway Station. As the world's first global superpower, the country had an image to live up to, and even a provincial police headquarters had its role to play. No expense was spared during the design and construction of the building, and although by the late 1980s this grand old lady was starting to show her age, she could still turn heads. A cross between the Palais de Versailles and Castle Greyskull, Warrington nick is to this day a place that any well-bred gargoyle would be proud to call home. She was not, however, looking her best that rainy autumn evening as Owen and I made our way across the yard, in through the back door and across the vast expanse of the parade room. Warrington's parade room was a cavernous hall that was big enough for the force football team to train in during inclement weather. In fact, it was probably big enough for the Red Arrows to train in.

Owen and I had been summoned by DS Lloyd for a meeting in the CID office, and I was not anticipating a pat on the back and a commendation. We made our way up the stairs, trying to remain as upbeat as was possible under the circumstances.

"Well, whatever happens, they can't reduce us in rank," said Owen reassuringly.

"No, just sack us," I replied.

"She's waiting for you in the DI's office," said DC Smith. "I suggest you put this down the back of your pants," he added, handing me a copy of the Warrington and District telephone directory.

As we approached I could see DS Lloyd silhouetted against the tall arched window, back towards us and arms folded.

We stopped in the doorway, and I coughed apologetically to announce our presence. After what seemed like an eternity, she turned around to face us and, without a word, beckoned us closer. I smiled like some kind of subservient puppy as we walked towards her. If I had had a tail, I would have wagged it – even fetched a stick or two if necessary.

As we got closer, I could plainly see by her facial expression that she was not actually angry; she was not annoyed or mildly upset. She was incandescent with rage. She was beside herself with fury. Her cheeks flushed, her eyes bulged, and she clenched both her fists. Like Mount Vesuvius, she was clearly about to blow, and there was no way that we were going to be able to outrun the lava flow. She took a deep breath and then, in a voice that could probably be heard throughout the building, began to list the breaches of policy and regulations which we had committed during our little afternoon out. I stopped counting somewhere around twenty. Then suddenly, she stopped talking and fixed us both with a stare which was unsettling in the extreme. By this time I would have gladly accepted fifty lashes and a substantial term of imprisonment with hard labour just to get out of that room.

"Well. What do have to say for yourselves?" she asked.

We looked at each other and then looked at her.

"Sorry, Sarge," we said in unison.

"'Sorry, Sarge'!" she shouted. "'Sorry, Sarge'? Not half as sorry as I am."

She looked at me, and I did the pathetic puppy thing again.

"Well, it's Friday night, we've had a long week, and I'm not going to waste any more time on you two idiots. I want your statements and a duty report on my desk by 9:00 a.m. Monday, so you're going to have to get your thinking caps on over the weekend. Now get out of my sight," she said.

"David!" she shouted as we reached the door.

"Yes, Sarge."

"Mr Morgan wants to see you at HQ Chester first thing Monday," she said rather worryingly.

Detective Superintendent Morgan was the senior officer responsible for postings to CID and was not the sort of chap to invite the likes of me to his office for tea and biscuits. He was the kind of man who could intimidate by his very presence, and frankly I expected the worst. To make matters worse, I had the entire weekend to look forward to our little tête-à-tête.

"Do you know what he wants, Sarge?" I asked, more in hope than expectation.

"I suggest you ask him on Monday," she replied.

Deep down I knew exactly what he was going to say to me. He was going to tell me that incompetent hot heads like me are not wanted on the CID and that I was being removed from the list of those qualified for appointment to the department. There is a tradition in the CID that failed detectives are sarcastically advised to "apply for traffic", but given my antics that day, I doubted that I would be welcomed with open arms to that department either. Things were not looking great.

I felt that the Prince of Wales check three piece suit made a bold statement, and I had no hesitation in adding it to my wardrobe in anticipation of becoming a detective constable.

Beautifully cut with hand-stitched lapels, I felt it was the height of sartorial elegance. Now, however, waiting outside Detective Superintendent Morgan's office, I was resigned to the fact that this would probably be its first and last outing. The little traffic light on Mr Morgan's door turned to green, and I knocked and entered.

"Good Morning, Sir," I said breezily.

"Come in, Gittins. Sit down," he said.

We're off to a flyer here, I thought.

Dilemma time straight away. Do I correct a detective superintendent, or do I just answer to the name Gittins?

"Right. You're qualified for CID, and you've passed the promotion exam to sergeant. It says here that you got trough your promotion board interview a couple of months back. Is that right?" he asked.

"That's correct, Sir," I replied.

"So what's the aim – promotion or CID?" he said.

"I'm not in any hurry for promotion. Ideally I'd like to get a few years CID experience first," I replied.

"Well, Gittins," he continued.

"Actually, it's Griffin, Sir," I interjected.

"What is?"

"I is. I mean I am. Griffin, that is. Not Gittins. Sir."

"Whatever," said the super.

Gittins it is then.

"There's a vacancy for a DC at Ellesmere Port, and I'm putting you forward for it – okay?"

This was more than okay. This was fantastic news. I had presented myself at the Detective Superintendent's office fully expecting to be measured up for a traffic warden's uniform, and now I'm being offered a DC post. Despite the Keystone Cops catastrophe of the previous Friday, I was going to become a full-time detective, and the great British public were to get the benefit of the Prince of Wales check. Everyone wins.

"Yes, Sir, that's great. Perfect. Thank you," I said gushingly.

Mr Morgan picked up his phone.

"Get me DI Holt at the Port," he barked. "David. I've got Gittins here with me. I'm posting him to you from next Monday to fill that vacant DC spot."

I backed out of the office bowing, scraping, and wringing my hands in an unintentional Uriah Heep impression. I was a little concerned about the Gittins thing in case it was a case of mistaken identity. But no, that was definitely my file he had in front of him. Maybe he just prefers the name Gittins, in which case I would happily change my name if that was what was required. In fact they can call me Englebert Humperdinck, Pippy Longstocking, or Cheever J Loophole if they so wish, so long as I get the job. Best of all, he hadn't even mentioned the events of the previous Friday, so I'd obviously been worrying unnecessarily.

I jumped into my car, turned on the ignition, and tuned the radio into *The Chart Show – Wuthering Heights* by Kate Bush. Can my day seriously get any better?

It wasn't until Kate launched into a second chorus of "Heathcliff, it's me Cathy, come home now" that it hit me and the depression set in.

Of course Mr Morgan hadn't mentioned my role in writing off three CID cars and attempting to strangle an innocent man. He knew nothing about it – yet. As soon as he found out what had gone on, it would be back to HQ for Gittins and down to the stores for the traffic warden's suit. I suddenly began to appreciate just how irritating Kate Bush's high-pitched warbling can be. For mercy's sake, *shut up, woman!*

They say that no news is good news. I have often wondered just who "they" are and why they say all these things. I have a mental picture of a group of professors, philosophers, clerics, and general clever dicks who meet in the great hall of some castle somewhere, probably in the Scottish Highlands, and sit around saying things which are recorded by some minor government official using quill and parchment. Anyway, on this occasion no news was exactly what I wanted to hear. I had spent all week awaiting the call from Mr Morgan's secretary informing me that the offer of a DC post at Ellesmere Port had been withdrawn, but I had heard nothing. I had checked the incoming post tray several times each day, double checking to see if there was anything for Gittins, but the bad news hadn't arrived. It had been a good five days for the squad, with some notable arrests and none of the stock car racing antics of the previous week. DS Lloyd had made no comment to Owen or me about our indiscretions, and she was overheard to say that the writing off of the three cars had proved to be a blessing in disguise. The squad had taken delivery of three new cars, and Owen and I had become minor celebrities amongst our colleagues. It was the science teacher's white coat all over again, but without the letter from the headmaster. We had arranged to have a beer after work at the Bear's Paw in Frodsham, and as I downed a chilled Holsten Pils, I dared to believe that the storm had passed. Hope springs eternal, at least that's what they say. You see – they're at it again!

As the newest DC in the office, I was not exactly bottom of the pecking order, as at any given time there were always two CID aides on attachment. There were, however, still some subtle signs of my lowly ranking in the batting order. There were eight DC desks in the main office, and one had been cleared and prepared for me. Like all the others it had three grey plastic trays – in, out, and presumably shake it all about. Unlike the other DC desks, however, mine had a telephone on it. It was one of four in the office, each of which was strategically positioned. One was on the front desk, from where the morning briefing was delivered by the DI; the remaining two were on the spare desk, which was used by the aides. Whenever a call was put through to the office, all four phones would ring simultaneously until one was answered by whoever was closest to it. The most senior DC always claimed the desk at the rear of the office, a short bus ride from the nearest phone. I think you're probably getting the picture. Anyway, what mattered was that I was there and that this was my desk and my phone. I had made it, and the Prince of Wales check was getting a well-deserved airing.

"Morning, Griff," said DS Dave Dennell breezily as he hung his green Barbour jacket on the back of the door.

"Morning, Sarge," I replied, standing up and offering my hand.

"I'm not big on the rank thing," said the Sergeant. "Call me Dave."

"Fine," I said. "You can call me Gittins." I explained to him about the meeting with the Detective Super, and it proved to be a good ice breaker.

Dave Dennell was without doubt the most laid-back cop in the history of the service: softly spoken with a lilting mid-Cheshire accent, totally unflappable and an absolute gentleman by anyone's definition of the word. Nothing seemed to rattle him, whether it was drug-fuelled knifemen throwing items of furniture from a first floor window, the sound of gunfire from a town centre pub, or an enraged DI demanding to know why a Crown Court committal file was not on his desk as instructed. Dave took everything in his stride with a wry smile and a shrug of the shoulders. Some people have the habit of inflaming a situation. Dave was able to calm the breast of the most savage beast by doing very little, or sometimes nothing at all. I have seen him quell a violent drunk by simply standing in silence as the man launched into a tirade of vitriolic abuse, and then Dave would place a fatherly hand on the shoulder and say quietly, "Anyway, son, come with me and we'll have a chat about it." Class.

My partner was Glaswegian DC Fred Reid, a unique character with a quick wit and a very well-developed sense of the ridiculous. Fred had specific responsibility for Neston and policed his patch with an evangelical zeal. He seemed to know all twelve thousand of the town's population by name and was a prolific thief taker. Everyone in the town knew and respected Fred, or Jock as he was commonly known. Prior to joining the police, he had served in the Scots Guards where, as a member of the Regimental Band, he had learned to play the drums. He kept a set of drumsticks in his office and would regularly relieve stress by drumming on the enquiry desk top while whistling regimental marches.

When Fred felt the need to do this, it mattered not if there was a member of the public at the desk. He would march out of his office, drumsticks under his arm, and commence his performance. On more than one occasion I have been obliged to suspend the production of someone's driving documents until Fred had completed his routine. When finished, he would place the drumsticks under his arm, say "Thank you. Carry on, Constable!" and march back into his office. Wonderful lunacy!

"Right, David, sit down" said Detective Inspector Holt as he opened my personal file on the desk in front of him.

"As you know, I wasn't involved in selecting you for this post, and you would not have been my choice," he continued.

DI Holt was known for direct speaking and didn't mince his words.

"However, you're here now, and I'll tell you exactly what I want and expect from you. I want hard work and total commitment. I will not tolerate coasting, just doing enough. It's not just about dealing with what comes in; it's about getting out there and getting amongst it. There's plenty going on in this town, and I expect my staff to be identifying target criminals and getting into their ribs. I've had a look at your file, and your arrest rate is as good as anyone's, but it's time to step it up a gear now. If that means long days, then so be it – you don't think about going home till the job's done. Any questions?"

"No, Boss. I'll give it my best shot," I said.

"Good," he said. "Oh, and by the way. This is for you." He handed me a brown envelope.

DS Lloyd's report into the car chase episode concluded with these words: "PC Griffin has worked extremely well during his time with the Burglary Squad, and his actions that day were typical of his enthusiasm. With hindsight it was ill advised to become involved in a pursuit, but I feel sure that he had the best of intentions. I have given the officer advice and restated force policy regarding pursuit, and I therefore suggest that the matter be marked off as 'No Further Action' and the documents be filed. I am aware that this officer is awaiting appointment to CID, and I do not believe that this isolated incident should in any way affect that decision."

So that was it. Having dealt with the matter by giving me an almighty bollocking she had then prepared a report which had effectively saved my fledgling CID career. I learned a number of lessons from her handling of this issue, lessons which I would put into practice when I achieved rank and, more important, responsibility for others. The one thing which troubles me to this day is that I never thanked her for what she had done. I always intended to, of course, but I never got around to it. Time passed, and the incident became a distant memory. Then Sheila died and it was too late. Or is it?

DS Lloyd was a first-rate detective, and her covert surveillance skills were exceptional. She is up there somewhere, probably watching, and there's every chance that she has eyeball. So here goes: Thanks, Sarge.

By pure chance Dave Dennell and I were virtually outside the door when we heard the radio message. Uniform had attended the scene of a violent domestic dispute and found a man with a single stab wound to the chest. He appeared to be in a bad way, and an ambulance was en route. Inside the ground floor flat the casualty lay on the bathroom floor, arms outstretched and shirt pulled open revealing a single half-inch puncture wound to the left of his breast bone. Dave headed for the living room to speak with our uniform colleagues while I knelt down next to the victim. There was blood all over the floor and on the back of the bathroom door. What little blood was on the man's chest, however, was already congealed, and none was coming from the wound. This was not a good sign, particularly as the site of the wound indicated that the blade may have gone through his heart. This would explain the severe and sudden blood loss. I felt for a pulse but could detect none, nor did he appear to be breathing. I looked into his eyes, and there did appear to be some vague recognition, but it was clear that his life was ebbing away. I decided that any attempt at resuscitation would only hasten his demise, so I just held his hand and spoke quietly to him as I heard the ambulance pull up outside.

The electrodes were placed on his chest, and I stood away as the power surged through his body. After a second attempt the paramedic placed a stethoscope on the man's breast and listened for signs of life. He shook his head and began packing away his equipment while his colleague completed the form attached to his clipboard. It is not the job of the Ambulance Service to remove dead bodies; that would be a matter for the duty undertaker, so the paramedics grabbed their kit and headed off to their next call.

While I had seen many dead bodies by this stage of my police service, this was the first time I had actually watched someone die. It had seemed like a very quiet and private moment, and I felt strangely calm, serene almost. I could not, however, afford myself the luxury of dwelling on the experience as Dave and I now had a murder to deal with. There was to be no protracted and expensive enquiry because the killer, the girlfriend of the deceased, was sitting calmly in the living room. Under Dave's ever watchful eye I organised the forensic examination of the scene and the meticulous evidence gathering process that would be required before we could present a case before the court. I arrested and interviewed the offender and put together the committal file, taking great professional pride in its content and presentation. With his gold–rimmed, half-moon glasses on the end of his nose, Dave went through the completed file with the proverbial fine-toothed comb.

"That'll do, son," he said, patting me on the shoulder before placing it in the DI's in tray.

Dave was always economical with his words, and sometimes it was necessary to fill in the gaps to make sense of his pronouncements.

"We don't cause any of this. We just sort it all out," he once said to me while I was dealing with a particularly vicious and unprovoked assault on a middle-aged man. What he meant was that we are not responsible for the terrible things which people sometimes do to each other, but we are there to try to make some sense of it all and to protect the weak and the vulnerable. Having done that, we should not be embarrassed to take a professional pride in what we do. At least, that's what I think he meant. On the other hand, he might not have meant anything. Who knows?

As the months went by, my confidence grew along with my experience, and even DI Holt appeared to be warming to me. More than anyone else, he was the one whom I most wanted to impress. DI Holt ruled his empire with a rod of iron, and no one took liberties with him. A fearsome character who could never be accused of courting popularity, he was a man whom you crossed at your peril. His authority was total, and I had tremendous respect for him.

He was the last person I expected to see as I sat in the police room at the magistrates' court waiting to give evidence in a burglary case.

"David, we've got a date for your ten-weeker," he said.

He was referring to the Home Office ten-week CID course which all detectives were obliged to attend and pass on appointment to the department. "You're going to Hutton Hall in October."

"Great," I said. "Thanks, Boss."

"You've earned it," he replied. "I've been looking at the figures, and your arrest rate is as good as anyone's. You've settled in well, and you're doing OK."

This was praise indeed from a man not noted for dishing out the plaudits. DI Holt had said I was doing okay. Over the coming years there would be other occasions when I would receive a pat on the back, but nothing ever beat this. Nothing came close.

My staple diet consisted of thieves, burglars, and bullies with armed robbers, con men, and even a couple of bigamists thrown in for good measure, and by the time October came along my arrest portfolio was starting to look quite impressive. Assuming I did well on my ten-weeker and passed the final exam, I was to become a tutor DC on my return, guiding CID aides through their six-month attachment. With ten years service under my belt, I felt I had finally achieved the credibility which I sought and life was looking good. Bring on the dancing girls!

On the outskirts of Preston, Hutton Hall is the headquarters of Lancashire Constabulary and home to one of six detective training schools in the UK. In October of that year the intake consisted of sixty detectives from all over the country, split into three classes of twenty. The ten-weeker had a reputation for hard work and even harder play, a concept which epitomised the ethos of the CID. The academic side included lectures on law, practice, and procedure, as well as intensive training in evidence gathering and presentation. There was instruction in the intricacies of forensic science, counterterrorism, international espionage, and serious financial crime. There were lectures from army bomb disposal experts, Special Branch detectives, the Security Service (MI5), the Secret Intelligence Service (MI6), and an assortment of other specialist speakers.

And if all of this wasn't enough to whet the appetite, then there was the prospect of consuming industrial amounts of alcohol every evening with trips out to many of the top night spots in the north-west of England. Chez Henry's would not be one of them.

My classmates proved a fascinating mix, with some real characters among them. Rob from Thames Valley and Richard from Essex were a couple of likely lads whom I quickly identified as potential soul mates, whilst Andy from the City of London Police was certifiably insane.

Each of the three classes had to appoint a social secretary whose job it was to arrange and organise the class's recreational activities, and Detective Constable Richard Shakespeare of Essex Police seemed the natural choice for us. He did not need asking twice. Each class was also expected to prepare and rehearse a song and dance routine which would become its signature performance at all social gatherings. Again, Richard was our man with a simple yet brilliant routine called "Running Bear". The routine involved Richard standing on a chair with the rest of us surrounding him in a circle. The lyrics, sung by Richard, told the story of the son of an American Indian chief who fell in love with a white girl. Our job was to perform a complex dance routine, expertly choreographed by Richard, whilst chanting the words "Umpa-eeka, Umpa-eeka, Umpa-eeka", which Richard assured us was grammatically correct Cherokee. Utterly insane, typically CID.

The other two classes were not to be outdone and countered with a Blues Brothers number, complete with sun glasses and trilby, and a Rocky Horror Show spectacular which breached numerous health and safety rules as well as some of the laws of gravity.

Whenever an outside speaker gave a presentation, all three classes got together in the lecture theatre, a large and impressive room with tiered seating arranged in a semicircular sweep. At some point during every lecture, we would perform a Mexican wave, to the total bemusement of the guest speaker. I will remind you here that these were not prepubescent schoolboys. We were grown men. I was in my thirties. We were, however, detectives, and that's what detectives do.

There was of course a serious side to all of this, and the amount of knowledge which we had to assimilate during those ten weeks was staggering. The studying was made all the more challenging because it was invariably done whilst suffering an almighty hangover and a blinding headache. Character building stuff.

Ten weeks passed in the blink of an eye, and I had sung, danced, studied, and drunk myself to the finishing post. Not all of our number had made it, some having failed the written exams and been returned to uniform duties. On the final evening there was a black tie dinner at Hutton Hall with speeches, presentation of awards, and of course song and dance routines. We put heart and soul into our "Running Bear" thing, and to this day I still get slightly misty eyed when I think back to that ludicrous performance. The final act of the show was the presentation of the course tie, a navy blue number with red diagonal stripes and small gold squirrels. The squirrel is the symbol of the Hutton Hall Detective Training School, and the course tie is worn with pride by detectives who have successfully completed the ten-weeker there. I still have mine. Somewhere.

Sometime around midnight the event came to an end, and hands were shaken, backs were slapped, and addresses were exchanged. Some great friendships had been forged during the course, and, in the tradition of these things, parting was sweet sorrow. It had been an intense and unique experience, and I felt a great bond with everyone in the room that evening. To this day the sight of a squirrel in my garden can still evoke powerful memories of those wonderful, crazy days.

All together now:-

Umpa-eeka, Umpa-eeka, Umpa-eeka, Ump …

Oh Running Bear, he loved a little white girl.

A fourteen-inch portable TV seemed a strange addition to the CID office, but there it was, sitting proudly in the far corner. Even more strange was the small keyboard, almost like a mini electronic type-writer, which was attached to it by a wire. Also wired to the TV was a piece of kit, which I later discovered to be something called a printer, and underneath the desk sat a white metal cube the size of a domestic washing machine. The man tasked with setting up our TV was a civilian boffin from something called the HQ IT Department, whatever that may be. He was a man of few words who seemed slightly irritated by Fred's questions, which were clearly distracting him from his duty. Neither Fred nor I had the slightest idea what IT was, but we were astute enough to realise that this was code for what was obviously some new crime-fighting tool to add to our growing armoury. It was all a bit cloak and dagger, and I for one was impressed by the way the boffin referred to the TV as "IT". Now, I'm not stupid and know that "IT" spells "it". Brilliant!

"Ah, Meester Bond, we have been expecting you."

With the job done, the boffin opened his flask and poured himself a cup of coffee.

"So what's 'it' for?" asked Fred with genuine curiosity.

"It's a computer, obviously, and it can do all sorts of things," was the reply.

It may have been obvious to him, but to Fred and me it was anything but. I had never previously encountered something which looked like a telly but wasn't.

"For instance, you can obtain a record of someone's previous convictions, which you can then print out and attach to a crime file," said the boffin. "Soon people will have their own computers at home – in time, most homes will have one."

This, of course, was absolute nonsense. I have always believed that it's a very fine line between genius and insanity, and clearly this man had crossed that line. In my childhood I had been a fan of an American cartoon series called *The Jetsons*. The Jetson family lived in the twenty-second century in a world where people travelled around in little gravity-defying bubble cars. I remember reading at the time that these flying cars would actually become reality and that by the 1980s we would be whizzing around town in them. I became fixated with the prospect of owning a flying bubble car and eagerly looked forward to the 1980s.

As the boffin unwrapped his crab paste sandwiches on the desk next to "it"', I looked out of the window at my clapped-out, knock-kneed, knackered Vauxhall Viva parked in the yard. Prepare for lift off!

Even if he proved to be correct and we did all have our own personal computer at home, why would I have any wish to print off lists of previous convictions in my living room?

Sandwiches finished, Fred and I prepared ourselves for the introductory lesson in the use if "it". Lunch, however, was far from over, and with great pomp and ceremony the boffin unwrapped a small pink French Fancy. Next up was an individual jelly, delicately eaten with a white plastic teaspoon, followed by a strawberry yoghurt. This was not so much a working lunch – more a children's party. All we were short of was a magician. Fred looked at me and shook his head.

Finally, the boffin wiped his mouth with a serviette and switched "it" on. After a short delay, presumably while the valves warmed up, we were happily printing off lists of convictions. This did seem an improvement on the old system, although I was determined not to appear impressed. Previously, pre-cons were obtained by telephoning the

Checro Department at HQ where the data was kept on paper records. I had visited that department and seen for myself the Dickensian system which had been in operation for a century or more. Handwritten entries were made in ledgers that would not have looked out of place in the offices of Scrooge and Marley. I had to admit that this was progress, but I would still have preferred a flying bubble car.

Having spent half an hour being shown how to use "it", Fred and I were expected to teach the other DCs, but I somehow knew that Fred's heart wasn't in it.

"I'll leave it with you, Griff," he said, and I don't believe that he ever touched it again.

The man sitting opposite me in the interview room had been arrested in connection with a burglary at the home of his friend's elderly parents. There was some circumstantial evidence to put him at the scene, and his fingerprints had been found near to the point of entry. However, because he had visited the house in the past, the forensic evidence was of limited value, so the interview was likely to prove crucial. I was to be the lead interviewer, and Fred was my second jockey.

Carl was a seasoned criminal with a string of convictions for theft, burglary, and assault, and mindful of his reputation for extreme violence, people were reluctant to give evidence against him. This was an opportunity to put him out of circulation for a while and to give the public a well-deserved rest from his activities, but we really needed an admission to be absolutely certain of getting him sent back to prison. From my previous dealings with the man, I considered that unlikely.

Carl always used the services of the same solicitor, Toby Reynolds, who was the senior partner in a local firm. Toby was by far the best criminal solicitor for miles around, and someone whom I would choose to represent me if ever I found myself on the wrong side of the counter. In reality, I could never afford to employ Toby because with his skills and experience, he did not come cheap. As a career criminal who had never done a day's work in his life, Carl had no such worries. The best representation that legal aid could buy was always on hand, courtesy of the taxpayer.

Although Toby and I were regular adversaries across the interview room desk, away from the police station we were quite happy to have a beer together from time to time. I once asked him if representing some of the lowlifes that came his way through the legal aid scheme presented him with a moral dilemma.

"Not in the slightest," he replied. "My job is to ensure that you do yours correctly. Yes, I will do my best to make sure that my client is properly and fairly treated, and I will exploit any failings on your part, but ultimately if a professionally represented client is convicted, then that is more likely to be a safe conviction."

Couldn't have put it better myself, I thought.

Toby wasn't the kind of brief who simply advises his client to make no comment. Depending on the circumstances and the strength of the evidence, it is sometimes in the suspect's interests to answer questions and cooperate fully in the investigation. On this occasion, however, Toby had correctly guessed that this was a "cough or nothing" job and had suggested that Carl should remain silent.

Having set up the tape recorder and gone through the

opening formalities, I began to question Carl. It may be useful to spend just a few minutes discussing how police officers question suspects in interview. Wherever and whenever possible, detectives will ask open rather than closed questions. A closed question is one that can be answered in one word, often yes or no. An open question cannot be answered with one word, thus encouraging the interviewee to engage in dialogue. For example, "Do you own a car?" is a closed question, as is "What colour is your car?" "Tell me about your car", on the other hand, is an open question. Do you see the difference? At first it takes a little practice to avoid closed questions, but it's well worth the effort because it's a far more effective way of gleaning information. Try it yourself in normal conversation and see what a difference it makes.

Cognitive interview technique is all about listening to the responses to questions. The effective interviewer will never interrupt a reply and will never begin to speak until the suspect has completely finished talking. The trick is to look into the suspect's eyes while he is talking, nodding the head slightly in encouragement. Even when you think he has finished, still do not speak; mentally count to ten before continuing questioning. This ten-second gap can be an unnerving void, and often the suspect will have an irresistible urge to fill it with more information.

Micro detail is a technique which can be useful in determining whether someone is telling the truth. For example, if you were to spend a couple of minutes sitting in a parked car outside a newsagents shop, you would notice dozens of tiny insignificant details which you could recount under questioning. Most, if not all, of these details could be verified to confirm truthfulness. The liar who uses this story as an alibi will know the name of the shop, maybe, but will not be able to provide micro detail.

Another useful ploy in the interview room is negative reinforcement. For example, if I say to you, "Do not think about a green elephant," what is the first thing you do?

We can use this principle by opening with something like, "Just relax and try not to worry about the evidence."

No sane detective would ever seek an admission from an innocent man; the truth is what we seek. Open questions, cognitive interview, micro detail, and negative reinforcement are just some of the tools in the detective's tool bag which can help in that search.

"Okay, Carl, I am going to interview you regarding a burglary last evening," I said in opening. "All we want is the truth, so just relax and try not to worry too much about this lot," I said, patting a brown folder containing the witness statements and forensic forms. "First, tell me what you know about the terraced house at 14 Seabank Avenue, Ellesmere Port."

Silence.

"Can you just confirm, can you hear me okay?" I continued.

Silence.

"Can you tell me about your friendship with Pedro Salgado?"

Silence.

"Would you tell me how you came to meet his parents?"

Silence.

"This is very important, Carl. Can you tell me how you know Mr and Mrs Salgado?" I asked.

"My client clearly doesn't want to answer your questions, so I suggest that we terminate this interview," said Toby.

"Your client is fully entitled to remain silent, Mr Reynolds," I replied. "Equally, I'm fully entitled to question him, and that is what I intend to do,"

There was just a hint of a smile on Toby's face as he continued to take notes.

The one occasion when closed questions are asked is at the end of a "no comment" interview when all other avenues have been explored.

"Do you know Mr and Mrs Salgado? When were you last at their home at 14 Seabank Avenue, Ellesmere Port? Did you break into that house last evening and steal cash and credit cards?"

Again, total silence.

Just as I was about to wrap things up, Fred placed a hand on my knee under the desk.

"Just a couple of things from me, son, before we – Pardon!" said Fred.

"What?" said Carl.

"I'm sorry, son, I thought you said something," continued Fred.

"No, I didn't," said Carl.

"You sure?" said Fred.

"'Course I'm fucking sure," said Carl.

"No need to swear, son."

"Sorry, it's just that –"

"Okay, must be me," said Fred, squeezing my knee.

"Yeah, sound, no probs, eh?" said Carl.

After nearly an hour of total silence, Fred had had got our man talking. Okay, he wasn't admitting anything, but it was a start.

"Right, Carl. Can I call you Carl, son?"

"Yeah."

To remain silent while someone is making direct eye contact and asking you questions is actually very difficult. Doing it for five minutes is easy enough, but try keeping it up for half an hour. Try doing it all day through a series of interviews, and it's mentally and physically draining. Anti-interrogation technique is something which military special forces practice for hours on end, and even well-trained professional soldiers sometimes crack during these exercises. Fred had sensed that Carl was struggling to keep it up and had finally got him to speak. The trick now was to engage him in general conversation for a few moments, something which makes it more uncomfortable to return to "no comment" mode.

"Okay, Carl, we won't be much longer now, and then we'll break for a cup of tea. Did you have breakfast?" said Fred.

"Yeah, it was crap," said Carl.

"What was wrong with it?"

"They're them microwave meals – they're shit," said Carl.

"I'll have a word with the head chef for you, son," said Fred. "Anyway, throughout this interview you've not answered any of my colleague's questions. That's your right, Carl, and I don't have a problem with that. Just before we wind things up, do want to change your mind and go through the questions again?" said Fred.

Silence.

"Okay, so let's just sum up then, shall we. At no time during this interview have you admitted any involvement in the burglary at 14 Seabank Avenue, have you, son?"

Silence and a smug smile.

"You haven't denied it either, have you?"

The smug smile was replaced by a look of panic as Carl glanced over his shoulder for moral support from his solicitor.

"You just want me to admit to something I haven't done," said Carl.

Fred placed both hands on the desk and leaned forward. "No son, never, ever admit to something you haven't done – that would be foolish. But be very, very careful before you deny something that you *have* done," said Fred, gently patting the buff folder containing the statements of evidence.

Forty minutes later we had a full admission in the can, and Carl was enjoying a microwaved lunch in his cell.

I took Fred back to Neston Police Station, where I prepared the remand file while he played the drums on the enquiry desk counter.

The village of Parkgate sits on the bank of what was once the mighty River Dee, which separates England from Wales. At the beginning of the eighteenth century, it was an important trading centre and port, providing a link between the land locked city of Chester and the open sea. It was a major embarkation point for Ireland, easily overshadowing its near neighbour Liverpool, and it was a popular tourist destination for the increasingly wealthy middle classes. During its heyday the rapidly expanding village played host to many national and international celebrities, including Lady Emma Hamilton and the composer Handel. Lady Hamilton, who was best known as the mistress of Lord Nelson, was born at nearby Ness and spent much of her leisure time bathing in the waters of the Dee at Parkgate in the belief that it would provide a cure for a skin complaint. Handel stayed at a riverside hostelry in the village during the summer of 1741, and it was here that he completed his famous *Messiah*.

One thing, and one thing only, prevented Parkgate from developing into a major city: mud. During the eighteenth and nineteenth centuries, the River Dee silted up, thus ending the port's aspirations to challenge the growing importance and influence of the city of Liverpool.

By the early twentieth century, what was once a mighty tidal river had become a huge grassy marshland, criss-crossed by narrow channels of water. During the 1980s Parkgate was home to just over three thousand people, its illustrious past confined to the pages of a few obscure local history books.

It was a bitterly cold winter's morning as I parked the CID car outside the Red Lion pub and looked across the marshes to Wales.

"What the hell are we doing here at this ungodly hour, Fred?" I asked.

"D'ye no fancy it, Griff?" he replied as we climbed out of the car into a biting, icy wind.

Fred was clutching a small piece of paper that bore a childish sketch of a section of the marshes and looked for all the world like a pirate's treasure map. It had been found in the pocket of a local criminal who had been arrested for handling stolen television sets, and Fred was convinced that it showed the location of more stolen booty buried on the marshes. I considered it unlikely in the extreme, but in a moment of weakness, I had allowed Fred to talk me into joining him on his crazy venture.

Fred was fully prepared for the arctic weather conditions with waterproof trousers, waxed coat, scarf, and bobble hat. I was wearing my prized Prince of Wales check suit and a thin cotton jacket, which would just about stand a stiff breeze on Oxford Street.

The marshland between the Wirral Peninsula and Wales covers several hundred square miles and is an extremely dangerous environment for anyone who is not familiar with it. Mother Nature has a unique talent for concealing deadly dangers in what looks to the casual observer like a benign, green, and pleasant land. When one stands looking across that grassy expanse, it looks perfectly possible to walk to Wales, and many have tried; most died in the attempt. Fred was fully aware of the perils posed by venturing out onto the marshes and had secured the services of an expert. Geoff was a member of the Dee Wildfowlers and knew the marshes intimately. Like all experts, he also looked the part. With a weather-beaten face, wiry grey hair, and a beard in which you could comfortably conceal a brace of pheasant, he was clearly born to do this. He wore a full set of waterproofs and a sou'wester and would have looked equally at home on the deck of a North Atlantic trawler.

Having made our introductions and exchanged pleasantries, Geoff gave us a brief resume of the many dangers that lurked just a few metres out from the sandstone wall in front of us. Deep, concealed channels of icy water; sudden tidal rushes; and evil, black mud that can trap the unwary like Mexican quicksand were all described with barely concealed glee.

"Cold can also be a major problem. Hypothermia, you know," said our native guide. "You need to be properly dressed and equipped." He eyed my three-piece suit and cotton wind cheater.

"Right, let's go through the checklist. Compass. Flask. Rope. Knife. Flares. Towels. Spare clothing."

My check trousers could be described as flares, so that was one out of seven for me, and I could already see the headline item on the evening news. If failing to plan really is planning to fail, then this mission was Operation Certain Death. We then compared our two maps in an attempt to narrow the search area. Geoff's chart was ordnance survey, ours was Long John Silver.

Next to arrive was Derek the dog handler with his German shepherd, Heidi. Some years previously, while executing a search warrant in a block of flats, I had been bitten on the backside by man's best friend, and since then I had avoided involving the dog section in any police operation. It's not that I don't like dogs; in fact I'm something of a dog lover and have owned three during my life. I believe that they make wonderful pets – I just don't rate them as police officers. As a young child holidaying in Italy, I once captured and befriended a brightly coloured lizard which I found on the wall above my bed. Since then I have always felt an affinity towards reptiles and would quite like to own a boa constrictor. I just wouldn't have any wish to take it to work with me. That's all I'm saying.

"What's Fido going to bring to the party?" I asked Fred as Derek introduced himself to Geoff.

"They're good at finding stuff," he replied.

"Yes, sweaty criminals, drugs, explosives, things like that. But TVs?" I was cold, wet, and thoroughly depressed; my morale was rock bottom; and I was resigned to the fact that I was going to die. Once I had accepted that inevitability, I became quite relaxed about it, in much the same way that Captain Oates must have felt when he stepped out of the tent and into the blizzard. We climbed over the sandstone wall and set off in pursuit of Geoff, Derek, and Heidi.

I could be some time, I thought to myself.

We followed in Geoff's footsteps as though we were crossing a minefield, knowing that even the slightest deviation could lead to dire consequences. Geoff walked with an unusual gait, the kind of walk that I had seen on TV natural history programmes. Slightly hunched forward with knees bent, he looked as though he was stalking some unseen prey or avoiding the attentions of an invisible, man-eating predator. Every so often he would stop, raise his hand above his head, and squat down on one knee. I found this mildly amusing for the first ten minutes or so, but an hour into our expedition up the Orinoco, I was beginning to wish I had brought my elephant gun. Our route had been carefully chosen to avoid the water channels, so we constantly zigzagged, greatly increasing the distance we would have to cover. By this time, my suit was soaked, as was my cotton jacket, and my Italian handmade shoes were beyond salvation. The only thing that kept me going was the certain knowledge that I would soon drift into a hypothermia-induced coma and it would all be over. Heidi, on the other hand, was having the time of her life, and it was clear that Geoff considered this to be the best fun you could have with your clothes on. At the edge of a five-foot-wide water gully, Geoff did his Hiawatha thing again, kneeling down and raising his hand, and we stopped to take instructions.

"We can't go round this one, so we'll have to jump across. Everyone happy with that?" he said.

Ecstatic, I thought to myself.

Geoff was first over, followed by Fred. Derek told his dog to sit, and then he jumped across with surprising agility for a man of his stature. Heidi looked at me, tongue hanging out of the side of her mouth, stood up, and launched herself over the narrow channel to join her handler on the other side. I steadied myself, took a couple of steps back, and ran towards the gully. Considering I was in lounge suit and expensive leather shoes, this was always going to be more of a challenge for me than the others, but I gave it my best shot, leaping into the air like an Olympic long jumper.

When I was midflight Heidi, who had been sitting contentedly on the opposite bank, suddenly stood up and showed her teeth in a fierce snarl. Now, I know these animals are well trained and have been exposed to all manner of traumatic situations to prepare them for what they may face out on the streets. As pups, they are subjected to gunfire, dustbin lids being banged together, claxons, people shouting – that kind of thing. What Heidi probably hadn't encountered before was a soaking wet detective in a rather loud check suit hurtling through the air towards her. She clearly perceived this as a threat and was fully prepared to deal with it. I could plainly see the reception which awaited me on the opposite bank, but I was already beginning my descent in preparation for landing. In a damage limitation exercise I attempted a kind of midair pirouette, preferring to present my buttocks to Heidi's canine teeth rather than anything more delicate. I landed on the back of my left heel, and Heidi sank her fangs into the cold, wet flesh of my backside. Screaming and falling forward, I placed my right foot into a patch of the gooey black mud which Geoff had warned us about.

"What the F – – –!" I shouted, as Derek berated his charge for her indiscretion.

As I attempted to regain my composure, my foot sank further and further into the foul-smelling, sucking, black gloop. Geoff had been right about the mud; all attempts to free myself proved unsuccessful.

"Keep still," he shouted. "You'll only make matters worse."

Geoff began filling a large plastic bottle with water from the gully while reassuring me with tales of the slow and agonising death experienced by lone walkers caught in this half solid, half liquid substance. Having poured the water around the area where my foot and ankle had last been sighted, he instructed me to gently wiggle my leg while pulling my foot upwards. My foot slowly appeared, minus its shoe, and I fell backwards onto the sodden earth behind me. Any lingering hopes that my favourite suit might survive our little jaunt were now dispelled, and I busied myself trying to retrieve the missing footwear. Handmade Italian shoes do not come cheap.

"Forget it," said Geoff, handing me a towel, socks, and boots from his bag.

Removing my other shoe, I spent a moment or two appreciating the craftsmanship of the handstitching before hurling it into the gully.

"Addio vecchio amico!"

After another hour or so, we were in the general area where the stolen property could be, so out came the pirate's map.

Still mourning the demise of my suit and the loss of my best shoes, I did my best to appear enthusiastic as we paced out the distance between clumps of razor sharp marsh grass, following the trail to an area of spiky gorse.

After half an hour of fruitless searching, my thoughts were turning to the return journey and the eventual prospect of a hot bath. What idiot would consider hiding stolen TVs out here on the marshes? The whole thing was utterly preposterous. Fred being Fred, there was no way on earth that we could call a halt to this wild goose chase until we had thoroughly searched the area indicated on the map, so I went through the motions; I owed him that.

All of a sudden there was a totally unexpected development.

"Bingo!" shouted a delighted Fred, holding a black plastic bag aloft above the gorse. The bag contained TV remote controls, an assortment of wires and cables, and documentation from a recently burgled electrical store. There were no TVs, but that didn't matter. What did matter was that we could now prove a direct link between the man in the cells and the stolen property. We had our evidence, Geoff had honed his orienteering skills, and Heidi had thoroughly enjoyed her walkies. Happy days.

COMMENDATION

1002 Probationer Constable David George GRIFFIN

For intelligence, initiative and tenacity in pursuing a suspect and eventually arresting him.

At 2.45 a.m. on 4 January 1978, whilst following a vehicle along Sutton Way, Ellesmere Port, Constable Griffin and another officer realised that the vehicle had been reported stolen earlier that night. After a short chase, the two occupants abandoned the vehicle and Constable Griffin went in pursuit of one of them. An arduous chase ensued through a blackthorn hedge and a stream, and at times the officer found himself in water up to his neck. The chase continued up a 40/50 ft. high, slippery embankment and ended in a passageway between two houses. When his eyes had become used to the increased darkness, Constable Griffin saw the man lying down in the garden of one of the houses. The officer realised that a direct attempt to arrest him would result in the man running away over other gardens and possibly escaping, and therefore pretended to speak into his radio, saying he had lost the man. This ploy was successful and Constable Griffin was eventually able to arrest the offender who was later charged with two offences.

This arrest shows the very highest qualities of policemanship from a young, inexperienced officer with only twelve months service.

G. E. Fenn

Chief Constable

13 March 1978

My first commendation.

Mum was so proud!

Sergeant Griffin 1991.

On patrol.

Another Satisfied Customer!

Inspector Griffin presents American tourists with a
Cheshire Police helmet.

Sally and me when I received my Long Service Medal in
2000.

Controversy still rages to this day. Did Geoff Hurst's shot cross the line? A Russian linesman and a Swiss referee were happy that it did, and England took a 3-2 lead over West Germany in the football World Cup final at Wembly Stadium. The date was 30 July 1966, and England went on to score a fourth goal to become the first host nation to win the tournament since Italy thirty-two years previously. I was eleven years of age at the time and can vividly remember watching the game on our small black and white television at home and celebrating wildly at the final whistle. A little like the day that JFK was shot, everyone seems to have a memory of that fateful summer's afternoon, even those who have little or no interest in football. Sitting at my desk and reading a Metropolitan Police report more than twenty years later, memories of that great day came flooding back to me.

Murder enquiries are never closed, even ones that remain undetected years after the crime. The Met CID was investigating the murder of a hotel worker which took place on the day that Bobby Moore lifted the Jules Rimet Trophy, and a new lead had emerged. A married couple from Cheshire had stayed at the hotel that day prior to emigrating to South Africa. Enquiries to trace them at the time had proved unsuccessful, and they had never been interviewed. The reason the South African authorities had no record of the couple was that they had never gone there. At the eleventh hour they had had a change of heart and had returned to Cheshire, setting up home in the village of Willaston. If this were an Agatha Christie novel, then the couple would be the killers and the case would be solved. In the real world, however, this was more likely to be a TIE enquiry, meaning trace, interview, and eliminate.

"Can you come with me. Griff? I want to try that address

in Liverpool again, see if we can lift that Johnson fella," said Fred. "And we'll do the Willaston job on the way."

"Yeah, no problem," I said.

Willaston is a leafy suburb comprised of large detached houses set in landscaped gardens, and it is popular with wealthy professional people. The house we went to boasted a wide, imposing gravel drive flanked by weeping willow trees and carefully manicured lawns. We approached the front door, which was framed by two impressive Roman pillars, and Fred rang the bell. After what seemed an eternity, it was answered by an immaculately dressed woman in her late sixties.

"Sorry to trouble you, madam," said Fred, showing his warrant card. "We're from the CID, and there's something I think you may be able to help us with. There's absolutely nothing to worry about."

"Really?" she replied.

"Could we possibly come in?"

The lady made no reply, but it was plain that we were going to have this conversation where we stood.

"Well," said Fred, "we're investigating an incident which took place on 30 July 1966. Now, I know that's an awfully long time ago, but you may remember it as it was the day that England won the World Cup."

The lady held up her hand, stopping Fred midflow, and turned her head to one side.

"Darling!" she shouted. "There's a man at the door — something about a cup."

As you have probably guessed, we did not have our murderers.

What we did have, however, was a wonderful catchphrase which Fred and I would go on to use whenever we were required to relate a complicated story.

The issue here, of course, was listening skills, or the lack of them. Effective listening is a skill which all detectives must either have or quickly develop. Have you ever been introduced to someone, shaken their hand even, and then ten seconds later had no idea what that person's name was? If so, it's not because you have a memory problem; it's because you haven't listened. You've never actually created a memory in the first place, so there isn't one there to recall. A good detective needs to listen intently to what is said and to log information for future use. Here's a simple technique to help avoid forgetting someone's name seconds after having been introduced. Look the person in the eye, use their name when greeting them, and then make a mental picture which combines the name and face. For example, if you are introduced to someone called Ray, make a mental picture of him holding a torch and shining a ray of light across a dark room. The system is even more effective if you make the torch huge and imagine him waving it from side to side. You only need to make the mental picture for a fraction of a second, and it will be logged as a clear, easily retrievable memory. Practice it and try it out next time you are at any professional or social gathering. You'll be amazed how effective it is and how it quickly becomes second nature.

The M62 Motorway across the Pennines is a route which has always captured my imagination. As the global village continues to shrink, the bleak moors between Lancashire and Yorkshire are one of the last remaining wildernesses in England. They have an eerie beauty which is uplifting, and yet at the same time dark and sinister. It is a region which seems to make its own rules of geography, geology, and climate and which can become unwelcoming and intimidating with frightening suddenness. The bright morning sunshine had given way to inky black clouds which were just beginning to disgorge their payload as I passed the sign for Saddleworth Moor, a name forever linked with the diabolical deeds of Ian Brady and Myra Hindley. I was heading for Huddersfield to interview a prisoner who had been arrested by West Yorkshire Police in connection with a series of domestic burglaries. The man was originally from Liverpool, had family ties in Cheshire, and had left his fingerprints at two burglaries in Ellesmere Port. Because most of his criminal activity had taken place in Yorkshire, it was decided that I would charge him with the Cheshire offences and then leave the local police to put him before a court and make the remand application. A look at his previous convictions suggested that he would be receiving a substantial custodial sentence, and I suspected that he may be prepared to admit further offences which could be taken into consideration.

The CID office was a hive of activity that afternoon with phones ringing, people shouting, and typewriters chattering. Having never had any previous dealings with Huddersfield CID, I was not expecting to see a familiar face, so was taken aback when I saw Alfie standing in the far corner making a cup of tea. It was more than ten years since we had last met during the final evening at Bruche, but he had changed little during the intervening years and was instantly recognisable.

"Fancy a pint at the Highwayman?" I shouted.

Alfie put his tea down, frowned, and looked at me.

"Griff? What the hell are you doing here?" he replied.

I smiled and offered my hand but was surprised by the response. Alfie's smile was, at best, half-hearted, his handshake limp and unenthusiastic. This was not the cheeky chappie that I remembered, the gregarious, devil-may-care scouser with the infectious laugh and passionate disregard for authority. If the passage of time could extinguish the sparkle in those eyes and the fire in that belly, then there was no hope for any of us. My instinct was to ask him what was wrong, but this was neither the time nor the place. In any event, was it really any of my business?

It was clear that Alfie was in no mood for a trip down memory lane, so I explained the reason for my visit and was introduced to Sammy, the DC dealing with our burglar. Sammy handed me a copy of the West Yorkshire file to read as part of my preparation for the interview and showed me into an adjoining office. The file told a familiar story of a young man who had started offending in his teens and had spiralled into drug abuse, burgling houses to feed an ever increasing appetite for heroin. I took out my interview planner and began making notes, highlighting significant times and dates. Satisfied with my plan, I put the papers in order and was about to stand up when the door opened and in walked Alfie.

"What d'you reckon, then?" he said.

"Pretty straight forward, I'd say," I replied. "Gotta be good for five years."

"At least," agreed Alfie.

"Are you involved in this job?" I said.

"Oh, no. I don't even work here. I'm on the Robbery Squad; I just called in," he replied, pulling up a seat.

Alfie sat looking at me in silence for what seemed like an eternity, and I got the clear impression that he was going to tell me something deeply significant.

Eventually, he took a deep breath and began to speak. He rewound the clock more than twenty years and began telling me about his private life, something about which I knew absolutely nothing. When we had first met at Bruche, he had been unwilling to discuss his domestic circumstances, and I had never pressed him on the issue. Alfie was ten years older than I was, and I guessed that he had experienced some personal problems before joining the police, but that was his business. At no time did I expect him to bare his soul to me in the CID office at Huddersfield Police Station ten years down the line, but here we were, and if he needed to talk then I was prepared to listen.

At nineteen years of age, Alfie had married his pregnant girlfriend at a time when that was considered the only honourable course of action under such circumstances. Baby Simon came as something of a shock to the "Jack the Lad" bricklayer, and the responsibilities of fatherhood had not sat comfortably on his young shoulders. By his own admission, he had spent too much time at the pub and too little time with his wife and son. Simon's development from a baby to a boy passed Alfie by as he travelled the country working on building sites, and by the time the marriage fell apart father and son had become virtual strangers. When Alfie joined West Yorkshire Police, he truly was beginning a new life, leaving his home, his trade, his wife, and his son behind him. The Alfie whom I had met during initial training at Bruche had locked his memories away and had

had no contact with anyone from his previous life. That was how things had remained until his son turned up on the doorstep of his home in Wakefield as a nineteen-year-old. Reluctant to open up old wounds, Alfie had initially shunned Simon's attempts at reconciliation and sent his son away. When it became clear that Simon was determined to get to know his father, Alfie had relented. Simon became a regular visitor to his father's house, and for the first time they began to bond.

When Alfie reached this point in the story, he stopped abruptly and stared out of the window. I was desperate for him to continue but knew that he had to take this at his pace. As he looked across the room, his eyes welled up with tears, and he began to drum his fingers on the desk. The clock on the wall ticked loudly as he slowly gathered his composure.

"It's drugs, Griff. All down to drugs. He needs his gear, so he spends the morning screwing houses and the afternoon off his head on smack. It's not a choice, not anymore. The gear's in charge, not him.

I can't take any more, Griff," said Alfie, his head in his hands.

It wasn't until I looked at the front cover of the court file in front of me and reread the prisoner's details that it all suddenly came into sharp focus.

"This is your son, isn't it?" I said.

Alfie made no reply; none was necessary.

The twenty-two-year-old who sat opposite me in the interview room bore no resemblance to the blond-haired boy in the battered photograph shown to me by Alfie. The eyes, once shining with wild innocence in the early springtime of youth, were dull and without emotion. The cheeks, once chubby and florid, were now severe and angular, ravaged by the effects of hard drugs. The bony and sinewy hands could have belonged to an elderly, arthritic lady, and the skin looked as dry as parchment under the florescent strip lighting. It was a sight with which I was depressingly familiar: an empty shell from which a once vibrant soul had long since departed. This is the reality of "recreational" drug taking. Simon had fully admitted responsibility for the two burglaries where his fingerprints had been discovered, as well as five other similar offences. Resigned to his fate, he cooperated fully and provided as much detail as his memory allowed. He offered no explanation for his actions, nor did he show any remorse. Just as his father had wisely said, "The gear's in charge, not him."

"They're going for a remand tomorrow," said Alfie. "He's not going to get bail, and he's going down for five, at least."

"Have you had a visit?" I asked.

"How can I? I'm a copper," said Alfie, trembling with emotion.

"You're his dad, Alfie" I said, taking hold of his upper arm. "Come on."

Alfie stood in silence, head bowed, as the Sergeant endorsed the custody record with details of the visit.

"Take as long as you want, mate," he said as he hung the clipboard back on the wall behind him. "Your dad's here to see you," he said to Simon as he unlocked the heavy steel door.

I patted Alfie on the shoulder as he walked into the cell and then moved away out of earshot, not wishing to intrude on what was a very private moment. Twenty minutes later a tearful Alfie walked out of the cell and passed me without a word.

The time was approaching 9:00 p.m. as I drove back across the moors reflecting on an eventful and emotional day. Many so-called celebrities make comments which trivialise and often glamorise drug abuse. The world of popular music has a lot to answer for, with the lyrics of many songs seeking to make drug taking sound cool and exciting.

The next time you hear such a song, I want you to think of Simon.

This was another first for me. Never before had I driven a little red post office van or worn a postman's uniform. Admittedly, it was a little snug over the body armour, but nevertheless, I felt and looked the part. It was a pleasant spring morning, and I was headed for the small sub post office at Blacon, just outside Chester.

We had information that two known robbers from the Speke area of Liverpool were armed with a sawn-off shotgun and intended to attack and rob the postman when he made his weekly delivery to the post office. They had apparently travelled to a remote area of North Wales the previous week, where they had practised firing the weapon. The robbers believed that every Thursday the little red van delivered a large amount of cash to the branch to pay pensions, and they intended to snatch the money. Our enquiries confirmed that on his Thursday visit, as well as collecting the mail from the post box, the postman did indeed deliver a package to the branch. The fact that it contained stationary rather than cash was of no consequence. Clearly, the bad guys had done their homework, and the threat was credible. Inspector Grounds and Sergeant Farr from the Firearms Unit had been tasked with putting together an operation, and at 5:00 a.m. I sat in Chester CID office as the team was briefed. The manager of the local sorting office had been taken into our confidence, and the postman had been asked if he was willing to carry out the collection and delivery as normal, but for perfectly understandable reasons, he had declined. I was asked if I would like to "volunteer" my services as a postman, or "moving target" as Sgt Farr rather tactfully put it. I was dispatched to the sorting office to be kitted out. I was also given a crash course in how to unlock, open, and unload a post box.

These operations are never an exact science, and already things were not going to plan. We had details of the vehicle used by the robbers, and a surveillance team had scoured the area near to their home address in an attempt to trace it. There was no sign of the car, but maybe it had been placed in a garage or left with an accomplice elsewhere. The inability to trace the car was an inconvenience but was by no means a catastrophe. Another surveillance team had been watching the house where the two lived, with the intention of following them when they left, hopefully to collect the vehicle. They would then be tailed, and as soon as they got close to Blacon Post Office, the Firearms team would carry out a hard hit on the car, and they would be arrested for conspiracy to commit robbery. If all went to plan, the chances of them getting to the post office and pointing a shotgun at me were remote.

Soon after midnight, however, one of the bad guys had left the address on foot while the other had been picked up by someone on a motorbike. The surveillance team did not have the staff to mount a double follow and had taken a gamble and stayed put, in the hope that the two would return. They had not done so, and now we had no idea where they were or if the job was still on. At the briefing, debate had centred around our two options. We could abort the operation and simply place uniformed staff in marked cars at high-profile locations to deter any attempted robbery. Alternatively, we could continue with our plan in the hope that we could spot the offenders' vehicle and pick up a follow as it approached the intended target. Cops being cops, the second option was the more popular choice. This course of action was, however, heavily reliant on the robbers using the car that was known to us. If they used another car, then we would have to resort to identifying the individuals – very tricky in a moving vehicle. All of this greatly increased the chances of them getting to the target and testing my body armour. Covert police body armour covers only the torso, leaving the head, limbs, and crown jewels vulnerable, so I was feeling a little exposed and nervous. It had been decided that I would not be carrying a weapon because I was to be surrounded by undercover members of the firearms team, all covertly armed.

"If it all goes belly up, Griff, just hit the deck, and we'll shoot over you," shouted Sgt Farr, to muted laughter. He wasn't joking.

"If you get killed, can I have your Barbour jacket?" added Inspector Grounds. He, on the other hand, was joking. I think.

I parked my little red van as close as possible to the post office, grabbed my khaki-coloured sack, and made my way towards the post box. I wanted to look and sound as much like a genuine postman as possible, so I decided to whistle, because that's what postmen do. (Any postmen reading this may disagree, in which case I stand corrected.) And do you know what it was that I decided to whistle? Well, I'll tell you. I decided to whistle the theme tune from *Dad's Army*.

Who do you think you're kidding, Mr Hitler,

If you think we're on the run.

Getting into character was my way of controlling the nerves because I was feeling very exposed. On every previous occasion when I had been involved in a live firearms operation, I had been armed and wearing a covert radio ear piece. This time I was totally in the hands of my colleagues and was relying on them to protect me from harm.

We are the boys who will stop your little game.

We are the boys who will make you think again.

I placed the letters in my sack and made my way back to the van, where I removed the brown cardboard box from the passenger seat. I knew that if our robbers where on the scene, this is when they would make their move, so it was with some trepidation that I set off on the short walk to the post office. After a few steps I froze, as I felt a tap on my shoulder. Momentarily, I considered taking Sergeant Farr's advice and hitting the deck, fully expecting to hear the sound of rounds zipping over me. As I spun around, however, I found myself face to face with a little silver-haired old lady.

"Not a bad day after all," she said to me.

"No," I replied. "Turned out quite nice now."

"Can you put this in your sack for me please, young man?" she asked, handing me a letter. "It's my grandson's birthday tomorrow."

"Well, we certainly can't miss that, can we," I said, taking the small white envelope from her.

In the hope of looking like a friendly postman rather than a jittery undercover cop, I chatted to her briefly, but my instinct was to tell her in no uncertain terms to go away. If the bad guys were going to strike, this was the moment, and I doubted that the lady was wearing body armour underneath her cashmere cardigan. I bid her goodbye and carried on towards the post office with my box of goodies.

"Morning," I said. "Stationery delivery for you."

"Thanks," said the postmaster "I don't think we've met before."

"I'm new to the job – The name's Griff," I replied.

Two minutes later I was back in the van and heading towards police headquarters feeling relief and disappointment in equal measure. I was hopeful that the robbers had been spotted and arrested nearby, but part of me wanted them to actually get as far as pointing a weapon at me so that their intent could be in no doubt.

Back at HQ the team was in high spirits. The robbers had been arrested a short distance away from the post office, and a loaded shotgun had been found on the back seat of their car. My day as a post office employee was over, and Chester CID would deal with the two prisoners, so after a brew and a debrief it was back to Ellesmere Port and business as usual.

> So who do you think you're kidding, Mr Hitler,
> If you think old England's done!

The silence of the mortuary was disturbed only by the gentle hum of the refrigeration system. The air was heavy with the smell of disinfectant and formaldehyde as I made my way towards the two bodies lying together, each covered with a starched white sheet.

Without a word, the mortuary assistant reverently pulled back the cotton covers to reveal the faces of a married couple in their forties. Three hours earlier they had been chatting and smiling; now they were dead.

Sudden unexpected death is always terrible, but there was some small grain of comfort in the knowledge that they probably didn't see, hear, or feel a thing. Their car had been hit head-on by another vehicle overtaking on a blind bend at a speed in excess of eighty-five miles per hour, and they had died instantly. The speeding driver also died at the scene.

As I stood silently absorbing this scene of indescribable sadness, the tears ran down my cheeks, and I squeezed my father's hand. I was to have no responsibility for the investigation into this matter, nor was I even on duty. The lifeless bodies lying in front of me were those of my sister, Margaret, and her husband, Don. After a family visit, they had waved goodbye to my parents at around 11:00 p.m., and seven minutes later they were dead. Margaret and Don were two lively, vibrant, happy-go-lucky people who were just beginning a new chapter in their lives as their three daughters reached an age when they could fend for themselves. Having known Don since I was around five years old, I loved them both equally, and I struggled to comprehend how their lives could be so easily and so randomly snuffed out.

Having formally identified the bodies and provided a written statement, I took my father home, where he and I drank whisky until the sun came up.

I had volunteered to deal with the unpleasant yet necessary formalities surrounding this terrible event, and the following afternoon I made my way to Mold Police Station. I walked towards the front door, pausing momentarily to glance at the coat of arms. "Heddlu Gogledd Cymru – Yr Wyddgrug" (North Wales Police – Mold).

"My sister and her husband were killed last night in a fatal accident at Rhydymwyn. I've come to collect the property from the car," I said to the young female constable at the reception desk.

"Mr Griffin, is it?"

"That's right," I replied.

"I'm very sorry," she said, reaching underneath the desk top to retrieve a clear plastic property bag.

I signed the property card, put the receipt in my pocket, and headed out onto the car park clutching that pitiful sack of possessions. On my way home I drove past the very spot where the accident had taken place, and I could still see small pieces of broken glass glistening like jewels in the summer sunshine.

Margaret's white leather hand bag was heavily bloodstained, so I washed it thoroughly before taking it to my parents' house.

I sat holding my mother's hand as we went through the contents of the bag together, Mum examining each item tenderly. I removed a small white card from the bag, noticing that it bore my parents' address details. It was a payment card for a Christmas hamper, which I assumed was to have been a surprise present. I just managed to retain my composure and control the tears as I handed the card to my mother. She didn't.

There is a widely held belief that police officers become hardened to tragedy and that they are in some way better equipped to deal with personal loss. Maybe some are; I don't know. What I do know is that I was a total mess.

After a couple of days' compassionate leave, I returned to work in the vain hope that it would help take my mind off things, but nothing could have been further from the truth. Each day, the drive to and from work took me past the scene of the accident, and each time I noticed some other small reminder of that terrible event. On more than one occasion, I stopped and got out of my car to recover some small fragment of debris – pieces of windscreen rubber, a headlight bulb, part of a speedometer dial – all of which were placed in a small cardboard box which I kept in my car. The box became almost like a religious relic, providing my last remaining link to Margaret and Don.

I know now that this tragedy had pushed me close to the edge. I was near to breaking point and probably should have spoken to someone, but I didn't. To a degree, I felt embarrassed at how badly affected I had been. After all, I was a copper. My parents had lost a daughter and son-in-law, and my nieces had lost their parents, so why should I have the monopoly on grief?

In the days before bereavement counselling and family liaison officers, I suffered in silence, telling no one how I felt. Until now.

Thank you for listening.

After four years as a detective constable, I was beginning to think that I was ready to move on, and my annual appraisal interview presented the perfect opportunity to explore my options.

The Deputy Divisional Commander, Chief Inspector Brian Lammond, was well-known to me. We had first met some years previously when I was a probationary PC, and he was a newly promoted Sergeant. We had hit it off straight away, and now, despite the gulf between our ranks, I felt that I could speak openly and honestly to him.

"I still enjoy what I do, but I think I need a change, Boss," I said. "It's starting to become a little too comfortable. I need a new challenge."

"Well, you're qualified for promotion, and there's a slot for an acting sergeant coming up on D Block. How do you feel about a return to uniform?" he asked.

"When do I start?" was my reply.

"As soon as possible. They've been one sergeant short for nearly a month now. Are you up for it?"

So it was over to the stores at HQ to be kitted out with my new uniform, and then back to my desk to clear a mountain of paperwork.

"You doing the right thing, son?" said Dave Dennell.

"It's been great here, Dave," I said. "But I think it's time to go. I may be making a huge mistake, but I feel I've got to move on. Thanks for everything."

We shook hands, and not for the first time in my career, I felt a wave of emotion as I packed my personal kit into a couple of bags and walked out of the office.

I hadn't been entirely honest with the Chief Inspector when requesting a change of role. There was another, more personal reason why I felt that I had to move on.

My time in the CID had taught me a lot about policing, about people and about myself. It had also had a dramatic impact on my private life. Like all good coppers I was married to a nurse, and Mary was working hard to further her career, qualifying first as a midwife and then as a health visitor. After our daughter Emma was born, Mary went back to full-time work, and we soon discovered the realities of the so-called work life balance. For me, twelve-hour days were normal, and I started to become a stranger in my own home. I would routinely arrive home after midnight to find a note from Mary informing me that my meal was in the oven and that she had gone to bed. On one rare occasion when I did arrive home on time, my baby daughter began to scream and point at this unexpected intruder, and my dog bit me on the ankle.

It was not uncommon for a week to pass with us having no face-to-face contact, our only communication being scribbled notes stuck to the fridge door.

I was focussed, to the point of obsession, on my work, and I was becoming cold and uncaring at home.

It is often said that absence makes the heart grow fonder, but in our case we were drifting apart. When we were able to spend time together, our conversation was strained and awkward, often spiralling into argument at the slightest provocation.

It was a crisp, frosty November night when I pulled up on the driveway of our small cottage in the quiet village of Afonwen in North Wales. With the time approaching midnight, I did not expect Mary to be waiting up for me when I walked into the sitting room.

"It's not working, is it Dave?" she said.

"No," I replied. "I'm so sorry."

We agreed to put our marriage on six months' probation but nothing changed and no real progress was made. It was my fault and I knew it, but somehow I felt unable to alter my ways.

I knew that I needed a change, and a return to uniform provided that opportunity. Deep down I knew that my marriage was beyond salvation, but I felt that I had to leave the CID for a while and get my life back on track.

So for the first time in nearly five years, I would be patrolling the streets of Cheshire in uniform, but first I had some other business to attend to.

CHAPTER 5

Moving On

It was a bitterly cold evening as the top of the range Mercedes patrol car pulled out of the yard at Reutlingen Police Station. The driver, Dieter, spoke very little English, and because I spoke no German, we communicated in schoolboy French. I was one of a group of twelve police officers from Ellesmere Port spending a week with our German colleagues as part of the twinning arrangements between the two towns. The trip was coming to an end, and at the conclusion of our tour of duty, we would be returning to the log cabin where I and my colleagues were billeted for a farewell drink with our new friends. It had been a fascinating insight into policing in Germany, and much of what I saw and experienced had been remarkably similar to what I was used to at home. Apart from the language, the uniforms, and the overt carrying of firearms, there were more similarities than differences.

We headed out of town to give some passing attention to a large holiday complex, a kind of a German Butlin's, where there had been a spate of burglaries. The bubble that was the German Economic Miracle had burst, and towns like Reutlingen were starting to suffer rising unemployment for the first time in a generation. Reunification with Eastern Germany had led to a large influx of people, which was placing a strain on already overstretched public services. Groups of disaffected young men hung around the streets drinking, and violence was becoming a growing problem. Dieter explained to me that burglaries had increased by 200 per cent in the previous two years and that crime overall had almost doubled in the same period. The holiday complex had been badly hit, with people breaking into chalets during the evening and stealing TVs. As we talked I saw two young men climbing over a six-foot fence out of the camp. Dieter slammed on the brakes, and we set off on foot after the two lads. I grabbed one of them around the neck and wrestled him to the ground.

"Okay, matey, you're locked up on suspicion of burglary," I shouted.

He looked at me in bewilderment. Clearly, he had not expected to be manhandled by someone dressed as a British Bobby and then yelled at in some unintelligible language. Fair point, I suppose.

We sat them in the police car, and Dieter began questioning them. I had no idea what was being said, but my gut instinct was that they seemed like a couple of fairly decent lads. Apparently, earlier on during the week they had met two girls who worked at the holiday camp and lived on site. That night they had been to visit the girls but had been obliged to make a hasty exit when approached by a security guard. We verified their story, dusted them down, and sent them on their way. I offered my apologies in as many languages as I could think of, German not being one of them. I think that the German for sorry is "Enschuldigge" or something similar, but I didn't risk it just in case. I have often wondered whether they ever told anyone the story of being arrested, then de arrested, by a crazy British Bobby outside a holiday camp. Who would believe them?

Back at the log cabin we drank, danced, and sang until the beer ran out. Then we all shook hands and said nice things about friendship, camaraderie, and the international brotherhood of policing. I seem to remember apologising for the bombing of Dresden and giving my personal assurance that it wouldn't happen again.

I have always been fairly impulsive when it comes to making decisions. Many of the most important decisions in my life have been made on a whim, a policy which would horrify many. However, I have seldom regretted any decision I have made and have never felt the need to be more analytical. On the journey back from Germany, somewhat unusually for me, I did experience some self-doubt about my latest choice. I had voluntarily relinquished my CID post to return to uniform as an acting sergeant, and I wondered if on this occasion I had been a little hasty. On the positive side I had little time to ponder the issue, because after arriving back in the UK late on Saturday night, I was due to start my new role on Monday.

Having sat through hundreds of briefings as a constable, I knew the difference between a good one and a bad one. A good briefing was about motivating and inspiring the team, not just reading out the duty roster. Policing is a serious business, but that doesn't mean that it has to be done with a miserable face, and a bit of banter and humour helps to get people in the mood. This was to be the first time that I, as patrol sergeant, would take the parade, and I was keen for everything to go well. It was 1:50 p.m., ten minutes before the start of the afternoon shift, when I stood outside the parade room with the briefing folder under my arm. Two deep breaths and off we go.

"Right, team. Eyes down, look in."

Everyone knew that this was my first parade as a sergeant, and no one gave me a hard time as I went through the duties, beats, and refreshment times. After I summarised the crime and arrest returns, I felt it was time for something a little Churchillian.

"We're not badly off for staff today," I said, "so let's get stuck in and get amongst it. Let's have plenty of stop checks and loads of intel reports. Look after each other, and if you think you might need backup, shout up early – don't wait till you're in trouble. Okay – let's get stuck in."

I know that in the great scheme of things my little briefing was no big deal. But it felt like a big deal, and I believed it had gone well. I was pleased and relieved and knew, there and then, that I had made the right decision in accepting this post. Like my first arrest all those years before, this was a rite of passage and a major milestone on my journey.

I enjoyed the extra responsibility of the sergeant's role and felt comfortable with it straight away. With thirteen years' service I was hardly a high flyer, but I had no regrets about not being promoted sooner. With my experience of uniform, CID, and firearms operations, I felt that I had laid solid foundations for the future. As patrol sergeant I was attending incidents, making decisions, giving advice, planning initiatives, and dealing with the professional and personal issues of my staff. The position of acting sergeant can be something of a poisoned chalice because any mistakes can jeopardise the chances of substantive promotion, so it was with some relief that I reflected on my first few weeks in the role. I had not dropped any serious clangers, and the team had done me proud with some excellent arrests.

By 1991 Cheshire Constabulary had sold off most of its police houses, so the choices on offer for a homeless and newly single officer were limited. 29 Churchfield Road, Frodsham, however, was available for immediate occupation. A substantial three-bedroom family home with a large garden, it was no one's idea of the ideal bachelor pad. I did, however, feel some excitement as I opened the front door and stepped into the spacious hallway. Having been unoccupied for over a year, the place was as cold as Baltic warehouse, with not a stick of furniture or a curtain in sight. The previous occupants had even removed all of the carpets, leaving bare floorboards with a lethal perimeter of spiky gripper rods. The ground floor consisted of a kitchen of generous proportions and two huge reception rooms. Outside the back door there was an alleyway giving access to an impressive array of adjoining outbuildings, one of which appeared to be some kind of medieval dungeon with a single wooden bunk. Cosy was not a word which sprung to mind.

Upstairs were three good-sized bedrooms and a family bathroom. Because all of my possessions were contained in one leather hold all and two black bin sacks, it was clear that clutter would not be a problem in my new home. Minimalist chic would be the order of the day, with no unnecessary embellishments. I made a note of the things I needed to buy to make the place habitable and quickly realised that my limited budget was likely to be a problem.

Friends had rallied around, and I had been promised a fourteen-inch portable TV, a set of plastic garden furniture and a clapped-out sofa bed, so I calculated that with the addition of living room carpet and a couple of sets of curtains, my dream home would be complete. Using a tape measure which I found in one of the outbuildings, I set about measuring the windows of the lounge and master bedroom. Work complete, I sat on the bare floorboards of the lounge and surveyed my new abode.

"Things could be worse," I said to myself.

Having just taken the morning briefing I was at my desk going through my in tray when the phone rang.

"Sergeant Griffin," I said.

"Morning, David. Chief Superintendent Ingman here."

"Morning, Sir."

"I'll get straight to the point," he said. "Your promotion has been confirmed, and you're being posted to Widnes Division. You start at Runcorn on Friday. Congratulations."

"Thank you, Sir, that's great," I replied.

Lying 15 miles to the south of Liverpool the town of Runcorn is probably best known for its impressive bridge, opened in 1961, linking it with Widnes. Spanning the River Mersey and the Manchester Ship Canal, it is the world's third longest steel arch bridge. Today it is one of the busiest stretches of suspended roadway in Europe with up to one hundred thousand vehicles a day passing over it, eighty feet above the water. The town itself is considerably older than its most famous landmark, having originally been settled by the Anglo-Saxons and named Rumcofan, meaning wide bay. It was the coming of the industrial revolution which saw the first major development of Runcorn, with chemical production companies identifying its location as ideal for their industry. Toxic waste from the factories could be pumped directly into the fast-flowing tidal waters of the Mersey and would be quickly swept out to the Irish Sea. Also, there were large tracts of flat land where liquid waste could be poured into drying beds to soak away or evaporate. Today's environmentalists would, quite rightly, be horrified by these practices, but in the nineteenth century the world seemed a big place, and no-one believed that mankind's activities could do any lasting damage. In the 1960s work began on the development of Runcorn New Town, and the architect Sir James Stirling was commissioned to design a revolutionary, state-of-the art housing complex providing low-cost, energy-efficient homes for working people. Maybe Sir James, like me, had been a fan of *The Jetsons* because "Southgate" was startlingly futuristic. Other equally modernistic housing estates sprang up in what had previously been a green and pleasant land, and the names of Castlefields, Palacefields, Murdishaw, and Windmill Hill appeared on the new map. The jewel in the crown of Runcorn New Town was the somewhat flamboyantly named Shopping City, a huge concrete and tile construction housing a covered retail park and numerous local government offices. The police station and magistrates' court were incorporated into Shopping City, and that was where I headed on a chilly March day to begin the next leg of my journey.

Max wasn't his real name. His real name was Glyn, but everyone called him Max – although no one knew why. Six foot two inches tall, fit as a race horse with a smile as wide as the River Mersey, Max was undoubtedly one of the characters of C Block. A former paratrooper, Max was keen and fearless and was exactly the kind of cop you wanted on your team. However, I had no idea who he was that first day as I walked towards the back door of Runcorn nick. Max was cleaning his patrol car whilst entertaining his colleague with an impression of the divisional commander, Superintendent Smith. As I tapped in the code to the security door, Max made his way over to me and clocked the three chevrons on my epaulettes.

First meetings are often monumental occasions, and the first words can be significant for a thousand reasons. Who can forget that first encounter in deepest, darkest Africa when Stanley enquired, "Doctor Livingstone I presume"?

"Hiya, Sarge. Do you know where the Hoover is?" asked Max.

This seemed a strange opener. This was my first day, and I thought I'd done quite well finding the police station. How on Earth could I be expected to know where the bloody Hoover was?

"No," I replied, probably a bit snottily when I think back.

As I walked up the stairs, the significance of Max's words suddenly struck me. Max didn't know me, but he knew I was a sergeant, and sergeants know everything, including the location of domestic cleaning appliances. This was an important lesson for me on my first day as a proper sergeant, and I vowed to myself that I would do everything I could to be worthy of this huge burden of expectation. Clearly I could not know everything, but I would do my very best to know as much as possible. I made a promise to myself there and then that I would strive to be the best sergeant that I could be.

The custody suite at Runcorn Police Station was typical of

the period: bleak and utilitarian. Like custody suites the world over, it had a very specific smell, a mixture of bleach, body odour, and tobacco. When I visited the custody area at Stuttgart Police Station, the first thing that struck me was that it smelled exactly like the cells in a British nick. I suppose I was expecting it to smell of Bratwurst and Sauerkraut, but no, it was bleach, body odour and tobacco. As well as a unique smell, criminals have something else in common: they all take two spoonfuls of sugar in tea. Every single one of them. It begs the question: does sugar have some effect on the human body which causes criminality, or does committing crime give you a sweet tooth? I remember one prisoner spitting out a mouthful of tea, saying "I don't take sugar!" I released him immediately.

At Runcorn, prisoners were brought in through the back door in the yard below and then transported to the cell area in a lift which looked like something from a Boris Karloff movie.

The journey from ground level to first floor was slow and laborious, with lots of clunking and grinding which only added to the slightly sinister, malevolent atmosphere. Inside the lift was a steel cage where violent prisoners were housed during the trip and I always felt that this slightly sci-fi entrance must have added greatly to the overall experience, particularly for the first-time customer.

As custody officer this grim and unwelcoming environment was my world, and I was responsible for the security and welfare of the detainees. I much preferred to be out and about as a patrol sergeant, but I knew I had to do my stint as dungeon keeper, so I vowed to do it with a smile.

It was shift changeover time, and John Chapman was going through the handover procedure, talking me through each prisoner's circumstances and explaining where each investigation was up to. Like me, John had recently been promoted from a DC's post and was serving his apprenticeship as a sergeant before a hoped-for return to CID duties. The handover complete, John passed me a cup of tea.

"What d'you reckon to this sergeant lark, then?" he asked.

"Early days yet," I replied. "What about yourself?"

"Hardly the realisation of a lifetime's dream, is it?" he said, glancing around our battleship grey world.

"Just another stepping stone on life's journey. I'm sure one day we'll look back on this with fond memories," I said, not entirely convinced myself.

"I'll bear that in mind," said John. "Always look on the bright side of life, eh?"

With that, I heard the unmistakable sound of the lift doors being opened down in the bowels of the building, followed by a tirade of foul Anglo-Saxon abuse and wild screaming. My first customer of the day.

I picked up a vacant clipboard and attached a fresh custody record to it in anticipation of welcoming my new guest. The lift clunked to a halt, and the heavy steel concertina doors opened with a screeching noise which always set my teeth on edge. Out walked a shaven-headed, tattooed young man flanked by two detectives. Restrained by a set of rigid handcuffs, the prisoner was clearly not pleased and was shouting threats of medieval violence at the two DCs, who were completely ignoring him and discussing England's chances of qualifying for the forthcoming European Football Championships.

DC Neil Burdekin explained the circumstances of the man's

arrest on suspicion of armed robbery, and I authorised his detention to allow the CID to investigate the matter. Having outlined the prisoner's legal entitlements, I advised him that he would remain handcuffed until I was satisfied that he posed no threat.

"Get fucked!" was his response, so at least we knew where we stood.

We placed him in a cell directly opposite my desk from, where I could supervise him whilst I put the finishing touches to the paperwork.

Admin completed, I made my way to the cell where our angry robber sat quietly on the bed contemplating his feet.

"Have you calmed down yet?" I enquired through the open hatch on the cell door.

"I shouldn't fucking be here," he said.

"Neither should I," I said. "It's shit. But we are here, so let's make the best of it, eh?"

He smiled and stood up.

"Fair point. Sorry, Boss. Can you take these off?"

"What's the magic word?" I said.

"Abracadabra!" he said with a smile.

"That's near enough. Put your hands through here," I said.

I removed the cuffs and gave him a pep talk about standards of behaviour and respect, to which he listened without comment. Hate the crime but don't hate the criminal, someone once said to me. Wise words in many ways, because I've always felt that hatred ultimately destroys the hater. Separating hatred of the act from hatred of the person is not always easy, but it's something I've always tried hard to do. Don't get me wrong, I'm no hand wringing, softy do-gooder when it comes to punishment, but I do accept that we are all the product of our upbringing, and it is sometimes useful to try to understand why people behave the way they do.

Here are some more wise words for you. Never judge any man until you have walked ten miles in his shoes. Then you can say what you like, because you're ten miles away and he's got no shoes.

For a middle-aged woman earning a little bit of extra housekeeping money by working evenings in an off licence, being threatened with a hand gun must be a deeply traumatising experience. There had been a spate of these offences over a six month period and our robber was the culprit. He had been picked out on an identity parade by several witnesses, an imitation self-loading pistol had been recovered from his home, and he had now admitted his involvement in nine robberies. Having been remanded in custody by the magistrates, he was to remain at the police station for three days while further offences were investigated. The slobbering, rabid psychopath of the previous day was now a model prisoner, and as long as his good behaviour continued, he and I would get along just fine. It was not my job to punish him; that would be a matter for the court.

While other prisoners came and went over the next couple of days, Joe and I got to know each other in the way that convicts get to know prison officers. Whenever I had a quiet moment, I would chat to him in his cell, and there developed between us a rapport and an understanding which may come as a surprise to you. If, however, you have ever been a police officer or a criminal, then you will not be in the least surprised. We spoke about childhood, schooling, family life, and many of the other day-to-day things which shape the way we turn out. At no time did I deliberately set out to counsel Joe, nor did I make any attempt to persuade him to confront his offending behaviour, but it was clear to me that he wanted to get some of this off his chest. So whenever I had a few moments, I would chat to him over a cup of tea. I knew from having seen his interview records that he had fully admitted the robberies and had also provided details of some other lesser offences about which we had no evidence other than his admissions. He told me that for the first time in his life, he wanted to put all this behind him and change his ways. He seemed genuine, but I would not be counting those chickens. He was going to prison for a long stretch, and a lot would depend on how he came through that experience.

Having completed the handover to the night shift, I went to speak to Joe to say goodbye; he was due for transfer to prison the following morning. He asked if I could spare him a few minutes, so I unlocked his cell, walked in, and sat next to him.

"I just wanted to say cheers, Boss. All my life people have treated me like shit – my mum, my dad, my stepdad, social workers – everybody. They told me I had to respect people, but they treated me like dirt. You've treated me with respect," he said. "Nobody's ever done that before. Nice one."

As I shook his hand, he bowed his head and began to cry. I patted him on the shoulder, stood up, and walked out of the cell.

I stood to attention as the Union Flag–draped coffin was carried slowly, reverently to the waiting hearse. I was wearing best uniform, helmet, and white gloves and had made a special effort with my boots. Two hours of gently buffing the toe caps with small, circular strokes had achieved the mirrorlike military style finish that was required. During basic training I had always hated bulling my boots, but I felt that for this occasion it had to be done. That's how Fred would have wanted it. Having served his country for the best part of forty years, first as a soldier and then as a police officer, it seemed so unfair that he hadn't enjoyed the long and happy retirement that he so richly deserved. He had died of a heart attack and he was gone.

As I stood outside the church, I remembered all that he and I had been through together over the years, and I thought that the world would be a less interesting place without him. Strangely, Fred's death so soon after retirement hadn't come as a total surprise to me. Deep down, I always knew that he was not the type of person who would experience old age and the frailty which comes with it. Healthy living, exercise, and moderation were never high on Fred's agenda, and I don't believe that he ever expected, or indeed wanted, to receive that telegram from the Queen.

"Better to live five years as a lion than a hundred years as a lamb," he once said to me. These words weren't Fred's own; Italian Dictator Benito Mussolini had first uttered them during his rise to power during the 1920s. Not everyone's idea of a role model, I agree, but you can see where he's coming from. Fred had certainly lived his life as a lion, and now age will not weary him, nor the years condemn. At the going down of the sun and in the morning, I will remember him.

Memories flooded back to me as I drove back to work,

and I smiled as I relived some of our shared experiences. I had lost a friend, a colleague, and a mentor, and yet this wasn't a time for tears. We had worked together, drank together, and laughed together, and he would always have a special place in my head and my heart.

I had been seeing Sally for a few weeks by now, and things were going remarkably well. She was a police officer, based at Ellesmere Port, whom I had first seen in the custody office almost two years previously. She had been sympathetic and supportive when I needed someone to talk to about my failed marriage, tolerating my sulks, tantrums, and mood swings. She listened to me without making judgement, and she made me laugh. She was also very beautiful, and I was falling in love with her.

"What's the score with the curtains Griff?" said Sally, a bemused look on her face.

"Bit of a cock up on the measurements front," I said.

Being new to the soft furnishings game, I was unaware that when buying curtains, you need a width which is at least double that of the window. I had bought a pair of drapes which exactly fitted the space, and so to close them they had to be pulled tight and secured at the bottom with drawing pins. The result was green and white stripy material held as tight as a drum skin – a look which I knew in my heart of hearts would never catch on.

As we stood silently admiring the tautly stretched polyester, a drawing pin, clearly unable to take the G forces, sprang from the bottom of the curtains and flew perilously across the room, narrowly missing my left thigh.

David Griffin

"Last orders at the Bear's Paw?" suggested Sally.

By the early 1990s we no longer used the Smith and Wesson .38 Special Revolver. It had been replaced by the Austrian-made Glock 9 mm Self-Loading Pistol, which packed a bigger punch and was a more up-to-date weapon. We also had the Heckler and Koch MP5, which the press delighted in referring to as a "submachine gun". This weapon could indeed be set to automatic fire, discharging a full magazine of 9 mm rounds in seconds. Ours, however, were limited to single shot or three-burst mode, which was more appropriate for police use. As I peered through the telescopic sight at the gunman inside the house, I used my thumb to move the small metal catch from the safety position to single shot. This was a life-or-death, shoot-or-don't-shoot situation, and the man's head filled my scope, red dot on his forehead. One gentle squeeze of the trigger, and a 9 mm round would crash through skin, skull, and brain, causing instant death. I felt cold and detached as I prepared to do my duty, but one thing made me hesitate. I couldn't actually see whether or not he was holding a weapon. From his posture and body language, I strongly suspected that the pistol was in his right hand at his side, but I couldn't be certain. Would it be right to kill a man without being 100 per cent sure that he was armed? But can I take the risk of allowing him to walk away out of my view? What if he then goes on to kill the boy, a death which I could have prevented?

"Visual contact with X-ray on the Black Face at one three," I whispered into my radio mouthpiece. "Yankee also in view. No weapon visible. Stand by."

In any police firearms situation, the decision whether or not to shoot is a matter for the individual and may be subject of intense scrutiny at a later inquest. Unlike in the military, no one was going to make the decision for me and issue an order.

I had always expected that in a shoot–don't shoot scenario, the choice would be made in a fraction of a second, responding instantly to an immediate and clear threat. This was something which we had practised endlessly during tactical training sessions and with which I was comfortable. This, however, was different. As the minutes ticked by, I had plenty of time to consider the level of threat and whether I would be justified in opening fire. My mind was made up.

I had the tactical advantage of a good firing point, with my weapon supported by the tree. I had the man in my sights and confidence in the accuracy of the MP5. I knew that I could put a round through his head without danger to the boy. I knew that I could squeeze the trigger before he could pose any real threat to me. Keeping both eyes open, I could maintain a sight picture on my target while still observing events in the kitchen. I made up my mind that if the man raised his right arm and the hand gun came into view, I would shoot him.

Then I watched. And waited.

Time can be very elastic. Forty-five minutes can pass rapidly when your football team is trailing by the odd goal, whereas when you're winning, two minutes of injury time can seem like forever.

Ten minutes spent watching a man through a telescopic sight, waiting for him to make a move which would signal the end of his life, feels like an eternity.

Eventually, man and boy walked from the kitchen and out

of my view. I relaxed my grip on the MP5 and reapplied the safety catch.

Had I made the right decision? Only time would tell.

"Your relief's en route to you, Sarge," said the voice in my ear piece. "ETA five minutes."

After three hours in position, I felt physically and mentally exhausted. It was with great relief that I handed over to Mark and withdrew from my observation point, crawling away towards a brick wall. Away from the potential danger, I stood up and stretched my aching spine. Having checked the safety catch on the MP5, I headed back to the incident vehicle, out of sight of the scene.

"Safety on – check. Point muzzle towards Kevlar unloading mat. Remove magazine. Cock weapon three times, discharging round from chamber. Check breach. Clear. Safety off – squeeze trigger – safety on. Weapon safe." I went through the drill in my mind as I had done a hundred times before.

"Thanks, Griff," said Smithy, taking the MP5 from me and placing it in the rack inside the vehicle. "There's a brew on."

Having been on duty almost eleven hours by then, I could have packed up and gone home, but I felt the need to stay in touch with events at the house. I was tormented by the possibility that I had made the wrong decision and was dreading the news that the boy had been harmed. It was past 8:00 p.m. before the ongoing saga finally reached a climax. As agreed between the gunman and the negotiator, the boy appeared at the front door of the house. He ran as fast as his little legs would carry him to the safety of a ballistic shield held by an armed officer before being reunited with his relieved mother. Seconds later the gunman surrendered at the front door.

"Stand still and do exactly as I say, or you will be shot," shouted Kevin, still pointing his weapon at the man from behind a black Kevlar shield.

"Place your hands on your head and begin to turn slowly around in a circle." This allowed a visual check to confirm that he was unarmed. "Now walk slowly towards me until I tell you to stop. Stop! Now lie down on your front with your arms stretched out above your head. Okay, good. Now place your right foot over your left ankle and keep completely still. Two officers will now come and search you. Do exactly as you are told, and you will not come to any harm."

Paul and Roger ran to him, Roger pointing his MP5 at the middle of the man's back. Paul placed the prisoner's arms behind his back, handcuffed him, and body frisked him.

As the offender was placed in the cage of the waiting personnel carrier, a three-man firearms team ran to the house to check and make safe. Seconds later two white-suited Crime Scene Investigation staff followed them inside.

It was a perfect, textbook end to the day. Job done.

As I drove home, I felt an enormous sense of relief that my decision and my actions had been vindicated. I had come within a whisker of killing a man, but I was happy that I had chosen not to do so. Whether that man has ever been able to confront and defeat his inner demons I don't know, but I hope that he has and I wish him well.

Conditions at "Chez Nous" were by now showing signs of improvement. The living room looked almost homely, with fitted carpet and some proper curtains. The promised sofa bed had duly arrived and took pride of place in front of the fourteen-inch TV. Admittedly, the white plastic garden furniture looked a little out of place, but it served a purpose and was easily tarted up with the addition of a table cloth and some seat cushions. Max had kindly donated a small, circular bamboo coffee table with a glass top, which gave the place a nice cosmopolitan feel. The kitchen now boasted a fridge, courtesy of Sally's Aunt Hilda, and a set of pots and pans bought from a car boot sale.

The rest of the house, however, still had all the cosy ambience of a disused aircraft hangar. Bare floor boards were still the order of the day throughout. With so much stripped timber on show, the hallway had a slightly nautical feel to it. All it was short of was a few deck chairs and a middle-aged man in a linen suit playing quoits.

The exposed spikes of the gripper rods still posed a serious hazard to pedestrians, and even a trip to the bathroom required stout footwear and a stick.

While *Ideal Home* magazine was never likely to come calling with the offer of a lucrative photo shoot, it was a happy house, to which Sally was a regular visitor. In fact Sally was so impressed by the living conditions, and the promise of yet more luxury to come, that she had agreed to marry me.

With a date set, we began looking for a house which we could buy together, and we arranged to view the quaintly named Frogmore Cottage just a short distance away.

The property was a small-end terrace house on the car park of The Chinese Delight restaurant and was just within our tight budget. Next door lived Eddie and Betty, the proprietors of the restaurant.

Immediately taken with the place, we went straight to the estate agent and made an offer. Three months later I locked the door to the police house for the last time and delivered the keys to the local station.

Sally and I moved into our new home and put the finishing touches to our wedding plans.

I'm looking for someone to change my life.
I'm looking for a miracle in my life.

"Question" by the Moody Blues. Possibly some of the most moving lyrics ever written. The words of the song seemed more haunting, more thought-provoking than ever, as I stood outside the front door of the small bedsit. The occupant of the flat hadn't been seen for some time, and the music of Justin Hayward had been playing continuously for twenty-four hours.

"Bravo Four from DS Griffin."

"Bravo Four receiving. Go ahead, Sarge."

"I'm outside the address now, cancel uniform. I'll make some enquiries and update you. Over."

CID would not normally be the first response to this type of incident, but I was nearby, heard the radio message, and decided to attend. Neighbours told me that the occupant was a man in his late thirties who had lived there for about a year and kept himself to himself. He was usually seen morning and evening when leaving for and returning from work, although no one knew where he worked. A check of the electoral roll had drawn a blank, and the landlord of the building was away on holiday, so we really had no idea who the man was. Unable to get any response to my knocking, I decided that there were sufficient concerns to justify forcing entry to the flat.

I felt around the edge of the door, and it appeared that it was secured solely by the Yale lock, so that was where I aimed my kick. The door flew open with unexpected ease and smashed against an internal wall, bouncing back against my leg. "Shit!" I muttered as I rubbed my throbbing knee.

The one room flat was sparsely furnished but immaculately clean and tidy. I was not in the least surprised to see a man lying face down on the single bed in the far corner of the room and knew immediately that he was dead. On a bed side cabinet next to him was an empty gin bottle and a packet which had once contained thirty-two Paracetamol tablets. Next to that was a neatly stacked pile of credit cards and a handwritten open letter, signed simply "Rob". I took hold of Rob's wrist in the vain hope of detecting a pulse, but his body was ice cold and waxy.

"Bravo Four from DS Griffin."

"Go ahead, Sarge."

"Police surgeon and duty undertaker please – one male deceased. Stand by for further details."

The letter told a heart-rending story of a broken marriage and a man unable to come to terms with his situation. His wife had left him to set up home with a work colleague, taking their two young children with her, and his world had been shattered. As I read the words, tears welled up in my eyes. I was an experienced detective with more than sixteen years service, and by this time I had witnessed many distressing and upsetting things. I had not, however, lost the ability to feel sadness, and for that I make no apology.

I have heard suicide described as a permanent solution to a temporary problem, and I wondered if, maybe given time, this poor man could have got over his sadness and gone on to live a happy life. I have also heard people describe taking one's own life a coward's way out, but I cannot subscribe to that school of thought. I knew little or nothing of this man lying dead next to me, but one thing seemed clear – he was no coward.

Tales of human tragedy are like leaves in a forest, and this was just one more sad story in an often unfair world.

I just wanted to share it with you.

In the mid 1990s Cheshire Constabulary employed almost 2,500 people, both police officers and civilian staff, and had an annual budget in excess of £60 million. Running an organisation of this size is a complex and demanding task, and any officer with aspirations of achieving senior rank needs to have an understanding of the principles of business management. Having passed my exams for promotion to the rank of inspector, and armed with a Higher National Certificate in public management and administration, it had been suggested to me that a couple of years at Force Headquarters would improve my prospects of advancement. I had mentioned this to Sally over dinner one evening, and unknown to me, she was on the case.

"Take a look at this," she said, sliding a print-out from Weekly Orders across the dining table.

"What is it? I asked.

"It's your next job," she replied. It read, "Quality Improvement Sergeant – Headquarters Management Services".

"Why would I want to apply for this?" I asked.

"Because it's exactly the kind of thing that you're good at, and the experience would be really useful for you when you go for the next rank," she said.

"What does it involve?"

"I've no idea," said Sally.

St Martin's Lodge was a magnificent Victorian mansion house set in landscaped gardens just one hundred meters or so from Force Headquarters in Chester, and that was where I headed on a glorious summer's day to face an interview panel. Preparing to be quizzed for a job I knew nothing about and, if I'm honest, didn't particularly want was a novel experience. Only a special type of masochist can really enjoy the gut wrenching, bowel loosening experience of sitting opposite an interview board, but on this occasion I felt surprisingly relaxed about the whole thing. Sitting outside Chief Superintendent Barclay's office with the very realistic hope and expectation of failure was a strangely uplifting sensation. I had just finished my coffee when the door opened and I was invited inside.

I was expecting the customary large desk shielding the stern faced panel members but was surprised to see three beige easy chairs in which sat Mr Barclay, Mrs Watkins (the force's senior civilian administrator), and Miss Holman form the Personnel Department. I was invited to sit in a black leather armchair, rather like the one from the TV series *Mastermind*, facing my inquisitors. On a small occasional table at my left elbow sat a jug of water and a glass. All very informal and welcoming.

After a brief exchange of pleasantries, Mr Barclay looked

me in the eye, cleared his throat, and launched into his first question.

"As you may know, you are one of five candidates for this post. The other four have all visited the department and spoken to staff in an effort to gain an insight into the workings of HQ Management Services. Can you explain why you chose not to do this?"

Disaster loomed. Straight away I had hit an iceberg and was taking on water. I was already listing to starboard, and it was only a matter of time before deck chairs began sliding over the side. My hastily put together response about wanting to approach the interview with an open mind convinced no one, myself included, and I was on the back foot. There followed an excruciating forty minutes during which I rambled, prevaricated, and generally made a fool of myself, to the obvious discomfort of the panel.

Back at Runcorn CID office, John Chapman handed me a cup of tea.

"How did it go?" he asked.

"Could have been worse," I replied. "If I'd turned up dressed as Ronald McDonald, broken wind really loudly, and answered several calls from my bookmaker on my mobile."

"Not confident, then?"

"I've more chance of landing a job as a ticket attendant on a Bulgarian nudist beach. Not to worry - probably wasn't for me anyway."

Although resigned to not getting the job, I felt embarrassed at having shown myself up in front of three people whom I knew and respected. *Oh well. C'est la vie,* I thought to myself as I made a start on my in-tray.

The call from Mr Barclay came rather more quickly than I expected, but I thought it was probably best to put the matter behind me and move on.

"David. We've completed the scoring from the interviews, and I have some good news for you. You came out in first place, so I'd like to offer you the post."

Tickets please!

My new role in Management Services Department was unlike anything else I had experienced during my police service. The hours were Monday to Friday, nine to five, which was a huge novelty. There was no unscheduled overtime to place a burden on domestic life and no bank holiday working. All in all, it was a breath of fresh air after almost twenty years of shift work, and I was enjoying the experience. The job itself involved researching a variety of topics, preparing reports, and making recommendations to improve the ways in which we delivered our services. It was also my first experience of working alongside some of the force's civilian support staff, who impressed me greatly with their professionalism and dedication. Working behind the scenes to deliver front-line services, these unsung heroes certainly put in a full shift, none more so than Karen Watkins, head of Management Services. Whenever there was a top level managerial flap, Karen would be hastily summoned to the fourth floor of the headquarters building for a meeting with the Chief and would sprint past my door at breakneck speed. I once suggested that if we were to issue her with a good quality pair of training shoes and install a fireman's pole outside her office, we could probably trim valuable seconds from her response time.

I travelled the length and breadth of the country visiting other police forces, as well as some private companies, looking at different working practices and how it was possible to deliver more without increased resources. On the often long train journeys, I read books by some of the "Quality Gurus" of the twentieth century and was particularly impressed by the work of William Edwards-Demming. He was an American academic who was largely responsible for helping rebuild Japan's manufacturing industry after World War Two. His ideas on continuous improvement and quality of service became the cornerstone on which Japan's incredible economic recovery was built.

As well as the research and development side of my new role, I also worked alongside Dr Ed Doran, a lecturer from Manchester University. The university was contracted to deliver training to senior officers in Cheshire, and Ed presented fascinating sessions covering such topics as problem solving tools and techniques, creative thinking and team dynamics.

Ed's delivery always held his audience spellbound and certainly made a huge impression on me, so it was with some regret that I assisted him with his last input to a group of newly promoted inspectors. The contract with the university had reached its end, and financial cutbacks meant that it would not be renewed.

"I've learned a lot from you, Ed," I said over coffee at the FTC. "Shame we have to call it a day."

"Thank you, David," he replied. "But maybe we don't have to pull the plug on the training."

"I'm not with you," I said.

"I could give you the package, and you could take it on – it's not copyright or anything; it's all my own work. Would you be prepared to do it?"

I was surprised and flattered that Ed would think me capable of delivering his training package. My experience of public speaking was limited to the odd best man's speech, and I had no training qualifications. Ed was a genius, a doctor of philosophy, a university lecturer, a supreme academic, a wit and raconteur. I, on the other hand, left school at sixteen with one GCSE and a certificate for swimming a width of Birkenhead Baths.

"I appreciate the vote of confidence, Ed, but you're one hell of an act to follow," I said.

"Nonsense. Come with me," he said.

We filled the boot of my car with Ed's lesson notes and overhead transparencies, shook hands, and went our separate ways. That was the last I ever saw or heard of Dr Doran.

Having spent hours reading, memorising, and preparing, I felt ready to deliver Ed's one-day input to the inspectors' course, but I felt that I needed to practice my technique in front of a live audience first. A half-day "Quality of Service" course for constables and sergeants provided the perfect opportunity.

Following Ed's example, I arrived early and set up the classroom with overhead projector, flip charts, and all the other props that I would require. I then went for a strong coffee to keep the nerves at bay.

Constables and sergeants with twenty-five years or more service are never the easiest audience, and a glance around the room suggested that this group would be no exception. I felt like a stand-up comedian about to debut at the Glasgow Hippodrome on a wet Thursday night.

To say that they were unreceptive to the concept of continuous improvement would be an understatement. I did my very best to capture and hold their attention, but what began as apathy soon turned to irritated contempt and finally downright hatred. At one stage I thought that they were going to start throwing things. Not the most auspicious start to my showbiz career.

"Just be yourself," was Sally's advice.

"That's how I lost my last job," as Bob Hope once said.

With our first child expected in November it was essential that we found ourselves somewhere bigger to live. Frogmore Cottage was barely big enough for two, so we had chosen a larger place and were busily trying to organise the move.

The Chinese Delight was one of the things we knew that we would miss when we moved. We had become good friends with Eddie and Betty and ate at the restaurant at least once a week. Both from Hong Kong, Betty spoke good English, Eddie less so. Conversations with Eddie were always interesting because I never really knew how much of what I said he understood. He always greeted me with, "Hello, Dave. Off today?"

I always replied yes, whether I was off or not, and that seemed to make him happy.

From our front door it was precisely twenty-seven paces to the restaurant, and on that rainy evening I was glad that it was no further. I shook the water from my umbrella, closed it, and placed it in the stand just inside the front door.

Sally and I approached the bar, where we were greeted by a smiling Eddie.

"Hello, Dave. Off today?" he enquired.

"Hello, Eddie. Yes. How are you?" I said.

Eddie didn't reply but smiled broadly as he prepared two gin and tonics while shouting instructions in Cantonese to one of the waiters. Betty appeared and joined Eddie behind the bar, smiling and waving as she saw us.

"Hello, you two. How's the house sale going?" she asked.

"Great," I said. "We've got a buyer, and everything seems to be going through without a hitch."

"That's good news, but we'll be sorry to see you go," she said with a slight frown.

Eddie continued smiling broadly.

"Management Services, Sergeant Griffin," I said as I picked up the phone.

"Hello, Mr Griffin. It's Carol from the estate agents here," was the response. "Bit of a hitch with the exchange of contracts. The purchaser has a cat, and there is a covenant imposed by your next-door neighbour which prevents cats living at Frogmore Cottage. The covenant dates back thirty years, so it was agreed long before your neighbour Mr Chu moved in."

"Okay. What's the solution?" I asked.

"Should be simple, hopefully. Can you speak to Mr Chu, explain the situation, and ask him to sign a form saying that he has no objection to the new neighbour owning a cat."

Sally was just weeks away from giving birth, and we could not afford any last-minute hiccups, so this issue needed to be addressed without delay.

I quickly drafted a typed disclaimer, and as soon as I finished work I went straight to my neighbours' house and rang the bell. Eddie looked surprised to see me because I had never before appeared on his doorstep. I was hoping that Betty would answer the door, or better still their daughter, Debbie, whose English was perfect. *Oh well, no time to lose,* I thought. *Here goes.*

"I need you to sign this form for me please, Eddie. You see, the previous occupants of this house didn't like cats, so they took out something called a covenant, which would prevent any potential buyer of my house from keeping cats. The lady who is buying my house has a cat, so we cannot complete the sale and exchange contracts until we have established that you and Betty do not object to your next door neighbour keeping a cat. So, if you could just sign here please, Eddie," I said, handing him the typed form attached to a clipboard.

Eddie looked long and hard at me. He then looked even longer and harder at the piece of paper on the clipboard. His usual friendly smile had been replaced by a concerned frown, a scowl almost. The thought suddenly struck me: maybe he does have a problem with cats, in which case the house sale is off, and we're in deep trouble.

After what seemed an eternity, Eddie's frown gave way to a broad smile, and he placed a hand on my shoulder.

"Hello, Dave. Off today?"

After my horrendous mauling by the constables and sergeants,

I was determined to polish up my act before entering the lion's den which was the inspectors' course. I spent hours in front of the bedroom mirror rehearsing my routine in the vain hope that I could emulate Ed Doran.

As it turned out, the newly promoted inspectors were a far easier audience and entered into the spirit of things enthusiastically. I went on to deliver six of the one-day sessions and found, to my surprise, that I quite enjoyed the adrenaline buzz of standing up in front of a class. I was also presenting half-day inputs on staff performance, development, and appraisal. All things considered, I was enjoying my time at headquarters, but I knew it was time to move on.

I felt strangely emotional as I sat all alone in the library at the Force Training Centre that spring morning, and my mind skipped back almost twenty-one years to my first day as a police officer. This could have been the very seat where I sat and studied that antique Occurrence Book and first became acquainted with Hemmingway's *Death in the Afternoon.* On this occasion, however, I was a little more focussed in my choice of reading matter. It was the morning of my interview for promotion to inspector, and I was working my way through a stack of *Police Review* magazines, hoping to pick up some vital snippet of information which could make the difference between success and failure. Having passed the written examinations and the promotion assessment process, I had no wish to fall at the final fence. Satisfied that I could not cram one more fact or statistic into my head, I replaced the magazines with the others and made my way downstairs for a last caffeine injection. As an interview candidate I was allowed access to the inner sanctum of the senior officers' mess rather than having to rub shoulders with the riffraff in the canteen. While plastic and Formica were considered suitable surfaces for the lower orders, inspectors and above enjoyed the unbridled luxury of heavy oak dining tables and walnut panelling. A picture of Her Majesty the Queen had pride of place on the wall, above a glass display cabinet housing some of the constabulary's silverware. Senior officers did not do self-service and a small team of waitresses weaved between the tables with jugs of coffee and silver tea pots. The atmosphere was one of restrained politeness rather than the raucous banter of the canteen next door. I chose to sit alone and continue my mental preparation rather than become involved in conversation, and my self-imposed isolation was respected. I suspect that most candidates behave in the same way, and no one in the room attempted to interrupt my solitude with small talk. At 10:45 a.m. I put down my coffee cup and made my way to the interview room, taking a seat outside the door to await my 11:00 appointment with an assistant chief constable and two chief superintendents.

Just over an hour later I was on the road heading back to Chester, feeling shell-shocked but reasonably satisfied with my performance. On reflection, one or two of my answers had been somewhat hesitant and unconvincing, but overall I felt that I had acquitted myself quite well. With two-thirds of my police career now behind me, the sands of time were rapidly running out, so a good performance was essential if I was to have any chance of climbing the promotion ladder. In any event, I knew that it would be a week or more before I received my letter, so it was best to put the matter behind me and get on with life.

On my way back to work, I stopped off at the estate agent's office, where I signed the last of the forms to complete the house sale. The covenant issue had been resolved, and our feline friend would be taking up residence within the week, so everything was falling into place nicely. Given the location of Frogmore Cottage, on the car park of a Chinese restaurant with a railway line to one side and a busy main road to the other, poor little puss probably had the life expectancy of a Battle of Britain pilot, but that was not my concern.

CHAPTER 6

Onwards and Upwards

Sergeant Griffin

You recently took part in the selection process for promotion to the rank of inspector. I am pleased to inform you that you have been successful.

I read those words twice and then retrieved the envelope from the waste bin to double check the name on it.

With baby George now added to the family, the pay rise which came with promotion, together with the enhanced pension, would be most welcome. Before the good news had fully sunk in, I had a call from Superintendent Worthington.

"Congratulations, David. You're promoted as of Monday, and you've been posted to Halton Division to work with Superintendent Hindle."

I knew of Peter Hindle by reputation, although our paths had never crossed. Those who had worked with him told me that he's not someone you would want as an enemy. As Divisional Commander he ran a tight ship and demanded high standards from his team, so it was with some trepidation that I entered his office in Runcorn Police Station on my first day as an inspector.

He was staring at his computer screen and tapping away on the keyboard as I walked in.

"Sit down, David," he said without looking up.

After a few moments he stood up, walked across to me, and shook my hand.

"Welcome to Halton Division," he said.

"Thank you, Sir," I replied.

"You're a member of the management team now, so it's first names, and mine's Peter. Okay?

"Thank you, Peter," I said.

"Right, come on," he said, grabbing a packet of miniature cigars from his desk and heading out of the office at a very brisk pace. I followed on with absolutely no idea where we were going, or indeed why.

Moments later we were in the station yard, just outside the back door. Peter lit one of his cheroots, and we set off on the first of several laps of the car park as he delivered a welcoming address in his inimitable style. He pulled no punches as he outlined exactly what he expected from me, and I took to him immediately. It had become increasingly fashionable for senior officers to litter their speech with management speak, a trait which I found immensely irritating. Peter was able to articulate his views clearly and concisely without ever once "touching base", "running it up the flagpole", "taking a time out", or indulging in "blue sky thinking". He spoke exactly the way a superintendent should speak and oozed common sense from every pore. He also looked the part: steely eyed and square jawed with the solid athleticism of a rugby league prop forward. If Hollywood should ever decide to make a blockbuster about my police service, then I believe that Clint Eastwood, complete with cheroot, should play the part of Peter Hindle.

That would make my day.

Uniformed inspectors are responsible for the day-to-day management of the sergeants and constables and for the provision of front-line policing. The maintenance of public order and community policing are the main functions of uniformed staff, while Divisional CID has its own separate command structure and terms of reference.

"Each of the inspectors also has two other specific areas of responsibility," said Peter, "and yours are contingency planning and traffic."

Traffic policing was something of which I had absolutely no experience, nor the slightest interest in. Also, having been directly involved in the writing off of three police cars earlier in my career, the irony of my new post was not lost on me.

"I look forward to the challenge," I said with as much enthusiasm as I could muster.

"I know that you have a CID background, and I'm told that you have an eye for detail and some good ideas," said Peter. "This is your chance to develop as a manager and show me what you can do."

Peter had a way of talking which commanded respect and inspired, and I was determined that I would not let him down.

I spent my first few days in my new role renewing old

acquaintances and making new ones as I went about my business. A lot of my time was spent in the familiar setting of the custody area, where I was responsible for reviewing the cases of detainees and overseeing investigations. When Peter and his deputy, Chief Inspector Mary Worthington, were not on duty, I was the senior officer in the division, and I thoroughly enjoyed the constant buzz of activity. I was making decisions, solving problems, giving advice, dealing with colleagues and members of the public, and fielding press enquiries, and I found the whole experience tremendously exciting.

With its many bars, Runcorn Old Town was a lively place on Friday and Saturday nights. When you put a few thousand people together in a relatively small area and add copious amounts of alcohol to the mix, the result is only too predictable.

It was our policy to put a high-profile uniform presence in the town to prevent and deter trouble, but we were limited by the numbers of staff at our disposal, and often the jam was spread a little too thinly. Also, officers were often called away to deal with incidents elsewhere, and when arrests were made detainees had to be transported to the police station, further depleting our numbers.

Despite our best efforts, it was always a struggle to meet demand between 11:00 p.m. and 3:00 a.m. on the weekends, so as night inspector I always did my bit by spending time around the trouble hotspots.

"Assistance required at El Greco's Restaurant in the old town!" was the call.

As I arrived I saw three men lying face down on the pavement outside the restaurant while officers handcuffed them. Yards away, a baying mob of drunken men were goading the cops. With the help of two members of the Special Constabulary, I began ushering the mob away with threats of further arrests.

"Assistance required outside the Bank Chambers – officers under attack," a voice shouted over the radio, and two patrol cars screeched away, sirens blaring and blue lights flashing.

"Report of a stabbing at the Kebab House in Regent Street. Ambulance in attendance. Any mobile free to attend?"

Two of my staff set off, sprinting the short distance to the late-night takeaway.

I went inside El Greco's to speak to the proprietor. The place looked like a Western saloon after a major gunfight, with broken crockery and smashed furniture littering the floor. I was surprised at the extent of the destruction, but then it was a Greek restaurant. People could have been smashing plates for half an hour before anyone realised that there was a problem.

I asked the proprietor whether the three men whom we had arrested were the main culprits, or whether any of the other group were involved.

He was happy that we had the right people, which was just as well because we had neither the time nor the personnel to carry out much of an investigation.

"Customer going berserk at the Indian opposite the Bank Chambers. Any patrol able to attend?"

"Inspector Griffin, en route," I shouted.

In the street outside the tandoori restaurant, a constable and a sergeant were attempting to restrain a spectacularly drunken man using a set of rigid handcuffs. We were all trained in the use of rigid cuffs, and they are normally a very effective way of gaining the compliance of a troublesome prisoner. When even a small amount of pressure is applied to the prisoner's wrist, the pain is intense and usually results in immediate cooperation. This man, however, seemed oblivious to pain and showed no signs of surrender. With a sudden and violent shake of his right arm, he wrested the cuffs from the sergeant and raised himself up onto his knees. With the KwikCuffs still attached to his wrist, he now had a formidable offensive weapon in his possession and posed a very real threat.

"Spray, spray, spray!" shouted the sergeant as he unclipped the CS gas can from his belt.

I turned my face to one side to avoid the liquid as a jet of CS hit our man squarely in his face.

Having experienced the effects of CS spray as part of the training, I know how unpleasant it is. There is an instant burning sensation, the eyes swell and close, and the nose pours. It is impossible to offer any further resistance once the spray has hit the target, and it is game over. This man, however, merely shook his head, blinked, and stood up.

It was time to resort to the old tried and tested technique which predated rigid cuffs and CS spray. The three of us leapt on our man and pinned him to the floor, paying particular attention to the wrist with the fancy bracelet attached. Crude but effective.

After a monumental struggle lasting some minutes, we managed to cuff his wrists together behind his back and overpower him.

"Thanks, Boss," said the sergeant as we placed our prisoner in the cage at the back of the personnel carrier.

We took cover behind the rear door of the carrier as a hail of beer bottles crashed around us, and I remember thinking, "There must be an easier way than this to make a living."

Back in my office, the sun was starting to come up over Shopping City as I totted up the score for the night. Twelve arrests in the old town for assault, drunk and disorderly, criminal damage, obstruction, and affray. A similar number of arrests across the rest of the division, including two in Widnes for attempted murder. With all our available cell space occupied, we had been obliged to lodge some of our prisoners at other custody suites across the county. It was going to be a busy morning for the early staff, who would have to interview, document ,and process more than twenty detainees.

I put the finishing touches to my night report and headed home.

Anyone making a complaint about the way in which they have been treated by the police was first spoken to by an inspector. The inspector's first job was to establish whether the person wanted to make an official complaint, in which case it would be forwarded to the Complaints and Discipline Department for a formal investigation. Some were happy for the matter to be resolved informally; others would withdraw the complaint entirely. If I felt someone had a legitimate grievance, then under no circumstances would I attempt to talk them out of making a complaint. I did, however, do my best to filter out the some of the minor, often unjustified complaints.

Mr Jeffreys was big fan of the complaints procedure. I never really understood how a man with no criminal convictions could come into contact with the police so frequently. Whenever officers attended an incident anywhere in Halton Division, there was a fifty-fifty chance that Mr Jeffreys would be there. That being the case, he was often questioned and his details were recorded. Whenever he was spoken to, he would make a complaint of harassment. If, on the other hand, he was not spoken to, he would complain that he had been ignored. Every complaint he had ever made had resulted in a referral to the Complaints and Discipline Department, and every single one had been found to be unsubstantiated. The bizarre thing was that whenever I had spoken to him, he didn't come across as being anti-police – quite the opposite in fact. He was always polite and cooperative and never failed to thank me for taking the trouble to speak to him. We would fill in the C & D form together, usually over a cup of tea in my office, and then he would make his way home before calling to register a further complaint about the manner in which the matter had been handled. I actually believe that complaining was his hobby.

His latest grievance concerned the arrest of a violent drunk outside the Talk of the Town nightclub. The prisoner had assaulted a doorman and was about to attack the arresting officer, who had used her CS spray in self defence. Mr Jeffreys was standing nearby and had apparently been affected by the spray. I did wonder what a sixty-four-year-old man was doing outside a nightclub at 2:00 a.m., but as Kim Jong-il of North Korea would say, "It's a free country."

"Good morning, Mr Jeffreys. Tea?" I said as I guided him to a seat in front of my desk.

"Please. Two sugars," he replied, making himself comfortable.

Denise, the Command Team secretary, nodded and backed out of the office.

"How are you today?" I asked.

"Never without pain," was his uplifting response.

"I'm sorry to hear that. Well, thank you for coming to see me. What can I do for you?"

I nodded sympathetically as he outlined the events of the previous evening, stopping only to examine the side of his face where he had been struck by "the noxious chemical substance". I could see no sign of the angry red inflammation which he so enthusiastically described. When he'd finished I expressed regret at his discomfort, told him what I could about the assault on the doorman, and explained why the officer had felt the need to use her CS. I then outlined force policy on the use of incapacitating sprays and reassured him that there would be no long-term effects from exposure to CS, although I advised him to see his general practitioner. Finally, I showed him my own CS canister and explained to him how it worked, which seemed to interest him greatly.

Safe in the knowledge that all the tact and diplomacy in the world would not divert him from his mission, I removed a C & D form from my drawer and began to fill in his details.

"I don't think that will be necessary, Inspector," he said, placing his hand on my forearm.

"I beg your pardon?" I said in shock.

"You've explained to me why the police lady had to protect herself, and that's fair enough," he continued.

I sat back in my chair and took a big gulp of tea.

"So you don't want to make a complaint?" I asked, still unable to come to terms with this totally unexpected development.

"No. I don't want to waste your time; I know how busy you are."

At that moment the station fire alarm sounded, clearly startling Mr Jeffreys. I was less startled because fire drills were a regular occurrence, and I remembered that we had been told to expect one that day. Fire drills were something which never failed to irritate me because they always happened at the most inopportune moment. Having said that, I can't think of a good time to stage one.

Of all the utterly pointless activities devised by mankind throughout the ages, fire drills would be in my top five – right up there with train spotting, bird watching, stamp collecting, and listening to the music of Barry Manilow.

Running screaming from a blazing building is not an activity which I have ever felt the need to practice. I count myself fortunate in that I have never been in any structure which has caught fire, but I'm confident that I would instinctively know what to do: leave.

Fire drill etiquette is also something with which I have always been deeply uncomfortable. Standing shivering in a car park for fifteen minutes making small talk while some busybody in a yellow jacket charges around shouting, "Has anyone seen Geoff from Admin?" never fails to get under my skin. Then there is the "all clear" pantomime, where we file obediently back into the building while the numpty in nylon smiles smugly at a job well done.

On this occasion I had the added burden of a professional complainant to look after. Fully aware of the paperwork which would be generated if I allowed Mr Jeffreys to burn to death in my office, I ushered him along the corridor, down the stairs, and out onto the car park of the council offices opposite the station. Once outside, I explained to him that the drill could take some time, so he may as well go about his business. We shook hands, and he thanked me once again before heading off in search of another opportunity to have his civil liberties abused.

It was about a week later that I received the forms from Headquarters Complaints and Discipline informing me that Mr Jeffreys had registered a formal complaint against me for my handling of the CS incident. Apparently, I had been dismissive of his facial injury and had thrown him out of my office. Part of me wished that the building really had been on fire and that Mr Jeffreys had been left tied to a chair inside.

Peter found the Mr Jeffreys story immensely entertaining as I showed him the C & D forms during one of our regular circumnavigations of the station yard.

"You're in the shit now, David," he chortled. "I can see you getting busted to sergeant."

"Thank you, Superintendent," I said. "I knew I could rely on your sympathy and support."

Peter flicked the stub of his cigarillo onto the ground, squashed it with the sole of his shoe, and kicked it into touch.

"Time for a brew," he said, slapping me across the back.

A little like DI Holt earlier in my career, Peter could never be accused of courting popularity. To many in the division he was a rather scary character and one best avoided if at all possible. While I had met some people who didn't like him, I never met anyone who didn't respect him. I respected him and I liked him.

Behind me was a small white tent surrounded by yellow and black striped tape. The body had been photographed, examined, and removed to the mortuary in readiness for a post-mortem examination, and now the Crime Scene Investigators were going about their business. Knife crime had begun to capture the headlines across the country and was becoming increasingly common on the streets of Britain's major cities. Although it was mercifully less common on the streets of Cheshire, it was still a very worrying trend which we were doing all in our power to eradicate. I had moved to a new role in the Press and Public Relations Office, where I worked alongside a small team of civilian press officers covering major news stories across the county, and I was preparing myself for a live TV interview. After a lengthy conversation with the DI leading the murder hunt, I was ready to face the cameras.

TV reporter Ralph Blunsom reread his notes before going through some last-minute checks with his cameraman. I had first met Ralph two years previously when he had given an input on media issues to the newly promoted inspectors course at the Force Training Centre. Ralph was and is the consummate professional, with a natural ability to put the interviewee at ease, and I was pleased that it was he who would be presenting the item. By this time I had given many interviews on TV and radio, but this would be my first ever live performance, and I was a little apprehensive. Recorded interviews are fairly stress free because any clangers can be wiped and redone. This was an altogether more daunting proposition; any mistakes would be beamed live into homes across the country.

At the back of my mind was the fear of sudden memory loss or, worse still, an unexpected attack of Tourette's Syndrome. Only days before I had watched a TV comedy sketch about a Tourette's sufferer at a job interview who, for no good reason, kept saying "arse". He didn't get the job. I know this is a totally irrational fear, but somehow I couldn't shake it off.

Ralph sensed my nervousness and took me to one side.

"Is this your first live piece to camera, David?"

"And possibly my last," I replied.

"You'll be fine. Just look at me and treat it as a conversation. After the first ten seconds you'll forget about the camera, and if you do trip over your tongue, just carry on regardless and don't dwell on it. The only person who'll notice any little blips is you, so relax. Always remember, I want this to go well, so I'm not going to give you a hard time. Happy?" he said.

Those few words of encouragement were priceless, and I felt surprisingly calm as a technician counted down from five to one on his fingers behind Ralph's head.

The interview went without a hitch, and my fear of live TV was dispelled once and for all. Newspaper and TV journalists often get a bad press, but in my dealings with them the overwhelming majority were professional and ethical, none more so than Ralph.

"Have you got a minute, Griff?" shouted Superintendent Pete Duffy as I unlocked the patrol car in the yard of Northwich Police Station.

He and I knew each other from my CID days when I was a DS and he was a DCI.

Supt Duffy was now Commander of the force's Operational Support Division and had responsibility for the firearms unit, dogs section, search teams, and air operations unit. The underwater search unit also came within his remit. This was a regional resource made up of officers from four police forces; Cheshire, Merseyside, Greater Manchester, and North Wales.

Although Mr Duffy and I had worked together in the past, we did not know each other well, and I had no idea what he wanted to speak to me about as I followed him into the building.

In the conference room he poured me a coffee, and we exchanged pleasantries.

"There's a vacancy coming up which I think would suit you. We need a new inspector to take charge of the underwater search unit. Interested?"

"Gut reaction – not remotely," I said.

"Don't be hasty, have a think about it," continued the Superintendent.

"What does the inspector's role involve?" I asked.

"Well, you wouldn't have to get your feet wet; it's management skills I'm looking for. I want someone who can effectively control the budget, increase productivity, and manage the amalgamation with the Lancashire and Cumbria team.

We're looking to create a new, six-force set up which would be the largest police diving and marine unit in the UK. There's also talk of putting air operations under the remit of the unit's inspector, so it's got the makings of a good job. What do you think?"

"Why me?" I asked.

"I think you'd do a decent job for us," he said. "You'd have to apply and be interviewed if you're interested. It'll be advertised across the four forces, so I don't know how much competition there's likely to be."

"I'll give it some thought, Boss. Can you give me a couple of days?" I asked.

"The advert will be in next week's *Orders*, and I'd like to see an application from you. I can't promise you the job, obviously, but I think it could be a good move for you."

As I drove home that evening, I mulled over my meeting with Mr Duffy. Uniform, CID, firearms, management services, press office, and now the possibility of underwater search and air operations. Is this the portfolio of someone with a wealth of diverse experience or that of a jack of all trades, master of none?

Sally listened intently as I told her about the underwater search unit job, my concerns, and my long-term hopes and aspirations. Having concluded her deliberations and taken full account of all the relevant factors, she had reached her verdict. "It's up to you, Griff," she announced.

So that's that sorted, then.

CHAPTER 7

Highs and Lows

As the inspector responsible for the Underwater Search Unit, I had an office at Runcorn Police Station, but most of the unit's business was conducted in "the van". This vehicle was a huge mobile command centre which provided the team's transport and also acted as equipment store, canteen, briefing room, and sometimes hotel. It was here that I met the team on my first day in my new role.

Bill was ex–Royal Navy and a vastly experienced diver, and it was he who greeted me with a mug of tea that morning. Of the eight divers who made up the team, five were former sailors or marines. We also had one female member, Sharon. Tea finished, Bill took it upon himself to give me a guided tour of the van under the watchful eye of Sergeant Ryan Reid.

"First things first, Boss, never ever call these flippers," said Bill, holding up a pair of flippers.

"So what are they, then?" I enquired.

"They're fins. And secondly, never, ever, ever call this an oxygen tank," he continued, while patting what looked remarkably like an oxygen tank with the palm of his hand. "It's an air cylinder. Last and most important, please don't call us frog men."

"Wouldn't dream of it," I offered reassuringly.

With these important ground rules clearly established, Bill became visibly more relaxed and continued his introduction.

An hour or so later, I got the team together in the conference room to explain my plans to control costs and increase productivity. I also outlined the strategy for the proposed merger with the Lancashire/Cumbria Diving and Marine Unit, which would mean increasing our staffing by five and inheriting more vehicles, equipment, and premises. I was aware of the danger of alienating my new team by giving the impression that there would be dramatic changes, so I tried to keep it low-key and avoided saying anything that I felt would alarm them. I can't be certain, of course, but I'm reasonably confident that they hated me.

I squeezed myself into the seat of the Soviet Air Force MIG fighter and took hold of the joystick. In front of me was a bewildering array of dials, controls, buttons, knobs, and levers. Little stickers with writing in Cyrillic script were stuck randomly on the bare metal surfaces, presumably to remind the pilot what to do and when to do it. I couldn't help thinking that if the pilot needed the help of Post-it notes while flying this contraption, then he was in the wrong line of work. I imagined firing up the jet engines and hurtling down the runway before climbing high above the North Sea to buzz NATO aircraft during the Cold War.

This particular piece of Russian hardware, however, was going nowhere.

Behind the barbed wire and electronic gates, just inside the entrance to the Cheshire Police Air Operations base, was a collection of a dozen or so derelict Soviet war planes. They had been bought for a knock-down price by a private collector after the collapse of the Soviet Union, with a view to restoration and display. For whatever reason, the restoration project had been abandoned, and these iconic pieces of aviation history had been left to the elements. Still bearing their original markings, they were in the same condition as the day they were decommissioned. Only the weapons systems and ejector seat apparatus had been removed.

The aircraft seemed sinister and malevolent under gun metal grey skies that autumn afternoon as I climbed out of the cockpit and down the rusting steel ladder. There was an eerie silence as I stood alone looking up at what, in its heyday, had been the most advanced jet fighter in the world. It seemed almost sad that this once cutting-edge piece of military kit was now reduced to sitting forlornly in some damp and dismal corner of a foreign field. As I stood gazing up at the red star markings on its wings, the heavens opened, and I sprinted the short distance to the prefabricated building which was home to the Air Operations Unit.

"Ah, Mr Griffin, good morning," said Phil. "Long time, no see."

Indeed, it had been a long time since Phil and I had worked together. We first met at Ellesmere Port Magistrates' Court, when I was a DC and he was acting as gaoler for the remand prisoners. I was waiting to give evidence in a robbery case, and our first conversation all those years ago had been cut short when one of the prisoners became abusive in his cell.

"Do excuse me for a moment," said Phil. "I have to go and suppress the working classes."

Phil was now an air observer, one of the three-man crew of the Islander Piston Prop aircraft operated by Cheshire Police. The pilots were not police officers, but civilians leased to us by a private company. The atmosphere at the unit office was reminiscent of the RAF bases featured in World War Two films, where Spitfire pilots with handlebar moustaches sat in wicker chairs reading *The Times* and waited for the call to scramble.

At the air base that day, Phil was engrossed in some admin task, busily shuffling receipts and invoices on his desk and making entries in a small green book.

"Look at this!" he exclaimed, handing me the monthly invoices for fuel and airport fees.

"Expensive business, flying. There's a popular misconception that it's the effect of air pressure and lift that makes an aircraft fly. Not true. What keeps a plane in the air is money – and lots of it.

"Then you get this lot doing their best to keep us parked up on the apron or, better still, in the bloody hangar," he said, handing me an edict from the CAA.

"That doesn't stand for Civil Aviation Authority you know. No, no, it's the Campaign Against Aviation."

The back seat of my car was covered with books, manuals, folders and box files as I drove home that evening. I had a lot to learn about police diving, as well as marine and aviation operations, and I had no time to lose. I would normally have put all that reading matter in the boot, but that was full of shoes.

I had been tidying up at home and had been amazed to discover just how many pairs of shoes and boots I owned. It's not that I had a thing about footwear; it's just that throughout my life I had never thrown a pair of shoes away. Every time I bought a new pair, it just added to the growing collection until it had reached saturation point. Trainers, pumps, walking boots, football boots, dancing shoes, romancing shoes, going out shoes, staying in shoes – you name it.

If, like me, you were a teenager during the seventies, you may remember a footwear classic – the stack-heeled clog. This was a leather masterpiece atop a three-inch wooden platform which made walking difficult and dancing to Tamla Motown hazardous in the extreme. I still had a pair in my wardrobe. Would I ever wear them again? Unlikely. I also owned a pair of brown hiking boots which looked as though they could have once belonged to an East German border guard.

Having loaded my collection into black plastic refuse sacks I had put them in the car intending to take them to the recycling bin on my way home from work. The thought of someone less fortunate than me being able to enjoy the incomparable pleasure of dancing to the Detroit Emeralds while wearing 3" stack heeled clogs gave me a warm glow. I stopped alongside one of the large steel recycling containers on the supermarket car park and opened the boot. As I approached the bin with my first sack, I was surprised at what I saw. Rather than just a hole to drop the shoes in, there was a kind of one-way shutter arrangement with a small handle on it. This allowed just one shoe at a time to be placed in the container, and it struck me as rather odd. It meant that the whole process was going to be somewhat time consuming.

I began loading the shoes one at a time into the tank, clanging the heavy metal shutter each time. As I did so, a car pulled up behind mine, and the lady driver gave me a withering look. I got the impression that she wished to donate some stilettos to the third world, and I was holding her up. As I continued about my business, her facial expression became ever more aggressive. I threw her a smile which said, "If you know a quicker way to do this, then feel free to help."

My final deposit, the mud-caked hiking boots, proved particularly difficult to insert into the small shutter and required a little persuasion and a lot of clanging.

Finally, my work complete, I gave the lady a smile and a wave and closed the car boot. It was then that I noticed the sign on the front of the recycling bin. In bold red capitals eight inches high, it said "THANK YOU FOR YOUR UNWANTED BOOKS."

Next stop was the petrol station. It was our wedding anniversary, and I did not want to arrive home without the obligatory bouquet of flowers. Yes, I know – flowers come from a florist, not a garage, but I just hadn't had time, so the garage it was. I have to admit that the choice wasn't brilliant, but the bunch with the stargazer lilies looked fairly impressive, and retailing at a whopping £7.99, I could not be accused of scrimping.

I carefully removed the sticky label which identified the origin of the blooms and placed them on the back seat of my car.

Reflecting on my day as I drove home, I smiled to myself

when I thought of the shoes incident. I would have plenty to tell my wife over our anniversary dinner that evening.

The beaming smile with which Sally greeted me at the door was soon replaced by a look of worried concern as she took hold of the bouquet. Knowing her love of stargazer lilies, however, I was confident that their heady, sweet perfume would soon win her round.

"Diesel," she announced with some authority after taking a cautious sniff.

"Nonsense," I insisted.

"These are from the garage, aren't they?"

"I've had a busy day, Sal," I offered in my defence.

"And they're DOA," she added.

"What?"

"Dead on arrival. Look," she continued, showing me a couple of wilted stems.

With the flowers consigned to the dustbin, it was off to the Chinese Delight, where we were greeted at the door by a smiling Eddie.

"Hello, Dave. Off today?"

Police diving is nothing like the kind of thing which you may have seen on TV programmes like *The Undersea World of Jacques Cousteau,* where coral reef and exotic tropical fish abound. Most of the unit's work takes place in limited, or sometimes zero, visibility and often in heavily polluted water. The waters in and around the UK are seldom much above freezing point, even in midsummer, and it takes a special kind of person to be willing to enter this hostile, dirty, and often dangerous environment.

As manager of the unit, one of my jobs was to risk assess requests for deployment and to authorise diving operations. I was assisted in this task by Sergeant Ryan Reid, a vastly experienced diver, dive supervisor, and former Royal Marine. Ryan was also a diving contractor, a qualification which I was also required to obtain. This involved a residential course in Newcastle, where I learned about the theory and physiology of scuba diving. Armed with my diving contractor's certificate, I worked alongside Ryan in ensuring that the unit's operations were carried out safely.

A significant part of the unit's work involved the recovery of dead bodies from water. The team routinely travelled between the Scottish border and Mid Wales to search for victims of homicide, as well as dealing with accidents and suicides. One successful operation in a Manchester city centre canal involved the recovery of a murder victim whose body had been cut into seven sections and encased in concrete. We also recovered the remains of sports divers who had died in the pursuance of their hobby, something which always reminded me and the team of the ever present dangers of scuba diving.

Constant exposure to harrowing and upsetting scenes can have a profound effect upon anyone, and the gallows humour of the team undoubtedly provided some relief from long-term emotional damage. Some may see it as callousness, but I would argue that it enables ordinary people to do extraordinary things in a cool, calm, and professional way.

The unofficial debrief in the van after completing a job was an opportunity to unload in a safe environment, and I believe that the humour and banter were essential parts of the process.

Superintendent Duffy had been right. This was a good job. I enjoyed almost total freedom to run my two units as I saw fit, and I was gaining invaluable management experience into the bargain. I worked with our legal department to draw up a consortium policy document to which the new six-force North-West Police Diving and Marine Unit would operate. With the support of Ryan and the team, I was able to reduce costs and increase productivity, and my efforts were being recognized. In my annual staff performance appraisal, Peter Duffy spoke in glowing terms about "creativity and innovation" and how I had achieved "significant results in a relatively short period".

Naturally, I was pleased and flattered to hear these words, though not as pleased as I was years earlier when DI Holt had said I was "doing okay".

With twenty-five years service, I was once again in my comfort zone, doing a job I enjoyed and working with people whom I liked and respected. While for many this would be the ideal situation, for me it felt like time to move on. I completed the application form for promotion to chief inspector and awaited the call to attend the selection process and interview.

CHAPTER 8

The Home Straight

I jumped into the taxi at Euston Railway Station, throwing my brief case onto the seat beside me.

"Thames House, please," I said to the driver.

"Where's that then, Guv'nor?" was the surprising response.

I had taken a taxi from Euston many times to dozens of locations across the capital and had never before been asked for directions by a London cabbie. These guys know everything; they've done " The Knowledge".

"I've no idea – I assumed you'd know," I said.

"It's a new one on me. What goes on there?" said the driver.

"It's the headquarters of MI5," I said.

"Got yer, Guv'nor, know it well. Didn't know it was called Thames House, though."

The route from Euston took us past Trafalgar Square and Buckingham Palace, as a talkative cabbie gave me a resume of his early life and career path. I got the distinct impression that he was trying to impress me for whatever reason. Maybe he thought that someone who hangs out with the Secret Intelligence Service was worth impressing.

As Detective Chief Inspector, Headquarters Crime Operations, I was responsible for community partnership issues and was in London for a two-day conference on international counterterrorism. More than two years after the terrible events of September 11, 2001, Britain was braced for terrorist attacks, and the purpose of the conference at Thames House was to examine how prepared we were to deal with such incidents. The list of speakers looked impressive, with inputs from MI5 officers, senior military personnel, and politicians. On the evening of the first day, there was to be a formal dinner in the mess.

Even for me, as a senior police officer and invited guest, gaining access to Thames House was no mean feat. I was questioned and searched at the reception desk while my brief case was examined and my warrant card and invitation carefully were scrutinised. I was then escorted through a security door in the reinforced glass screen which separates the foyer from the rest of the building. Once inside I was issued with a hologram identity tag, which I hung around my neck, and was escorted to a large hall where the delegates were beginning to gather.

Coffee machines and I have always had a somewhat uneasy relationship. I'm never entirely sure what I'm doing and am convinced that these contraptions can sense my uncertainty, in rather the same way that a dog can smell fear.

Obtaining a latte with sugar was proving problematic, so I was mightily relieved when Jeremy came to the rescue.

"Here, allow me, old chap", he said, reinserting my fifty-pence coin while pressing several buttons simultaneously. "Bit of a knack to this."

Unlike me, Jeremy clearly knew his way around a hot drinks dispenser, and in no time at all I was enjoying the unbridled pleasure of instant freeze-dried coffee and rehydrated milk powder.

In his midforties with salt and pepper hair and a cut glass Oxford English accent, Jeremy looked and sounded like a proper spy. With the simple addition of a black bow tie and a white tuxedo, he could have had a walk-on part in a Bond movie of his choice. During our introductions he made no secret of his secret occupation, but then why should he? The building was full of spies and spooks. He then handed me his business card, which surprised me greatly.

I looked across the room and spotted Detective Superintendent John Armstrong, a good friend and colleague from Cheshire. John and I had known one another since we were both young constables and had worked together on the CID. I had no idea that he was going to be at the conference, or else we would have travelled together on the train from Chester.

Having bid farewell to Jeremy the Spy, I just had time to greet John before we were herded into the seating area for the opening address by a brigadier from the Royal Marines.

Despite the seriousness of the subject matter the day was interesting and entertaining, with touches of humour. I got some insight into the tremendous amount of work that goes on day and night, both at home and abroad, to detect and disrupt terrorist activity. Someone once said that however effective and professional the security services are, they also require a huge slice of luck to prevent attacks. In fact, they have to be lucky all day, every day – while the terrorist only needs to be lucky once. With this sobering thought, we rounded the day off with a syndicate exercise simulating a terror attack by a group of suicide bombers. The day concluded with another input from the brigadier, summing up the lessons we had learned and reminding us, if any such reminder were necessary, that we live in a very dangerous world.

The dining hall at Thames House is an impressive room with high vaulted ceilings, almost cathedral like in scale. Long tables were set out with white linen, silver, and crystal.

As John and I selected our seats, I spotted Jeremy the Spy, who had changed into a white tuxedo and black bow tie. Wonderful!

Pate de fois gras was followed by pan-fried salmon with mint and cucumber rice. The choice of wine was limited to Shiraz or Chardonnay, but that suited me just fine. Chardonnay is my favourite grape and South Western Australia my preferred region of origin. The tipple on offer was a perfect buttery wine with hints of citrus and vanilla, finished and presented in a way that only the Aussies know how. Most of my fellow diners had opted for the Shiraz, so I polished off a bottle unaided before one of the waitresses discreetly placed another one in front of me. Not wishing to appear ungrateful, I made a start on the second bottle and was soon starting to feel the benefit of its 13.5 per cent strength. John was doing similar damage to the Shiraz, and we were soon giggling like schoolboys. I assume that there was a dessert and, in all probability, cheese and biscuits, but I can't say for certain because two bottles of wine and several stiff gins had taken their toll.

I vaguely remember an after-dinner speech by a superintendent but could not comment on its content or presentation. John mentioned a pub which he had spotted near to the hotel where he and I were staying, and we agreed stop off there for a nightcap. This seemed a good plan because we had clearly not had enough to drink.

As we staggered off in the general direction of our hotel, the cool evening air filled my lungs. The pavement seemed strangely spongy, almost like walking on a mattress, but we were on a mission. We needed beer.

If the English Tourist Board had set up a pub scene to epitomize everyone's stereotypical idea of a good old Cockney Knees Up, then they could not have done a better job. The jukebox was belting out "Chas and Dave's Greatest Hits" as a gaggle of revellers sang and danced around it. All we were short of was a Pearly King and Queen. In amongst the dancers I spotted someone I had spoken to earlier that day: Ken the DI from the Metropolitan Police. Drunk as a monkey, tie undone and cigarette wedged in the corner of his mouth, he was clearly having a ball. John and I headed straight for the bar; we hadn't had a drink for some twenty minutes and needed to make up for lost time.

Jack was from California and was also on a mission. He was the proud owner of a twenty-five-year-old Triumph Spitfire sports car which was currently grounded for the want of some engine parts, and had travelled to England hoping to pick up the necessary bits. Having booked into a small hotel opposite the pub, he had decided on a nightcap before bed. By the time he had told me and John a little bit about himself, the three of us were on our third pint and were the best of friends.

As a happily married man who had taken certain vows in the house of God, I was not the sort of chap who would normally be on the lookout for an extramarital experience in an obscure London boozer, but Elsie was a bit special.

On paper she was not the type of girl that I would normally go for because she was quite a bit older than me – probably in her late seventies. She had long black hair with wide grey roots and the look of a woman who had seen life. She was, however, an accomplished dancer, and I believe that we worked well together.

Through the alcoholic haze I seem to remember doing a Beach Boys duet with Jack, and I still have a niggling fear that I may have danced the tango with Ken, although I can't be certain.

One thing I do know is that by the time we left that pub, I was absolutely plastered. John assures me that back at the hotel we had another beer in the bar before retiring to bed, and he could be right.

I had absolutely no idea where I was or what time it was. Total darkness engulfed me, the type of complete, suffocating blackness which can only be achieved by heavy, expensive curtains. I slid out from under the duvet and headed to my right, crashing into some furniture and sustaining a painful injury to my knee. I hopped around the room until my hands touched the soft velvet of the window drapes, which I pulled open with a flourish. As the bright morning sunlight lit the room, I winced and stepped back, like Count Dracula awakened in his crypt. After a moment or two I again approached the full-length window and looked out. A red double-decker bus cruised past and a black Hackney cab stopped to pick up a fare on the opposite side of the road. There could be no doubt about it: I was in London. But how and, more important, why?

Reality slowly dawned as I cradled my aching head in both hands. It was clear to me that I had suffered a brain haemorrhage and had been admitted to some specialist hospital in the metropolis for emergency treatment.

Not being a member of BUPA, I was surprised to have a private room and impressed by the facilities on offer. I would not have expected a National Health Service hospital to run to this kind of luxury – plasma TV, tea and coffee, Internet point, and even a trouser press! And they say the NHS has no money!

It was clear to me, however, that I was seriously ill, so I climbed back into bed to await the medical team.

"Are we doing breakfast, Griff?" said a voice on the phone at my bedside.

I was amazed that the nurse sounded remarkably like John Armstrong and was disappointed that I would not be getting breakfast in bed. I was, after all, a very sick man.

As memories of the previous evening began to filter back into my addled brain, I realised with some relief that this wasn't a life-threatening brain condition; it was a hangover. It was, however, not just any old hangover. It was the mother, father, daughter, and step son twice removed of all hangovers, and I wasn't at all confident that I would pull through.

I staggered around the room gathering my clothing and my thoughts while avoiding any unnecessary head movements.

International counterterrorism, that's what this was all about. I was here to defend the realm against Al Qaeda, and I couldn't find my trousers.

At the coffee machine, Jeremy was again on hand to sort

me out with a latte. When I mentioned my head injury, he produced two small white capsules from a plastic container in his top pocket, assuring me that they would do the trick. I questioned the wisdom of taking two pills of unknown origin from a spy, but considered it a risk worth taking. If he'd accidentally handed me two deadly cyanide tablets, then I felt sure that they would do the trick equally as well.

I did my level best to enter into the spirit of things for the rest of the day, but I felt, and probably looked, like death. It wasn't until John and I jumped into the taxi taking us to Euston that I began to feel normal again and dared to hope that I just might survive.

We strolled along the platform, and John stopped alongside one of the first-class carriages with its fancy lighting and opulent seating. He greeted the guard and stepped inside.

"Where are you going?" I shouted.

"Chester, I hope," he replied.

As a superintendent, John was entitled to ride on the gravy train, while I, as a mere chief inspector, was booked steerage class.

I left John to enjoy his finger buffet, complimentary evening newspaper, and Indian head massage, and I settled down for a bum-numbing, two-and-a-half-hour journey back to the north-west.

My office was in the force's new headquarters building set in countryside on the outskirts of Winsford. As DCI responsible for community partnership, this wasn't exactly the hands-on detective's role that I was hoping for, but I had been promoted and I was determined to make the best of it. Until I had attended and passed a senior investigating officer's course I would not be able to lead a major enquiry, so I had to content myself with the endless rounds of meetings that my new job entailed.

My department had specific responsibility for issues such as domestic violence, abuse of elderly people, child protection, prisoner resettlement, crime reduction, and prolific offender programmes, so I wasn't short of work. As the police representative at various multi-agency meetings, I worked with other organisations to devise and implement strategies to reduce crime and improve public confidence. I was working alongside some very talented and committed professionals, and together we were able to deliver some good results, but I wasn't getting a buzz from what I was doing. As a DCI, I knew that my days of kicking in doors and wrestling people to the ground were largely behind me, but I still felt the urge to get involved in some real, practical police work from time to time. Whenever an opportunity presented itself, I did get involved in operational duties, but without my senior investigating officer's ticket, I was always the bridesmaid, never the blushing bride.

During an organisational reshuffle, my role was incorporated with another DCI's job, and I was invited to apply for that, or one of five other DCI posts. For no good reason, I decided to turn my back on the CID and apply for a job as a uniformed chief inspector on one of the three newly formed territorial divisions.

Cheshire was now divided into three policing divisions: Northern, Western and Eastern. Whatever happened to Southern Cheshire remains a mystery to this day.

I was posted to Northern Division where my old friend,

Chief Superintendent Nick Ingram, was divisional commander. Nick and I had first met when we both worked at HQ Management Services, and I was delighted at the opportunity to team up with him again.

Northern Area was made up of six towns, including my old base at Runcorn, and had its divisional headquarters at Warrington. Warrington was the biggest town in Cheshire, with a population approaching two hundred thousand, and it had hit the headlines across the world in 1993 when the Provisional Irish Republican Army singled it out for bomb attacks. On 20 March an unsuccessful attempt to blow up a gas storage plant was followed by the detonation of two bombs in the town centre on a busy shopping day. These blasts killed two young children; three-year-old Jonathan Ball died instantly, twelve-year-old Tim Parry five days later . During the police investigations into these events, Constable Mark Toker was shot in the stomach by a member of an IRA Active Service Unit and was lucky to survive.

The deaths of two innocent young children caused worldwide outrage and provoked widespread condemnation, both of the Provisional IRA and of terrorist violence in general.

Colin Parry, father of Tim, founded the Peace Centre as part of a campaign to try to reconcile communities in conflict, and today there are many links between the town of Warrington and Irish people on both sides of the religious and political divide.

For a relatively anonymous provincial English town, Warrington has made international news on a surprising number of occasions. Many older Americans will remember the town as the location of the United States Air Force base at Burtonwood. Formerly home to the Royal Air Force, during World War Two RAF Burtonwood became the largest USAF base outside of the United States. It was visited by many major celebrities, including Humphrey Bogart and Bob Hope, who stayed in the town while entertaining the GIs at the base. US involvement with Burtonwood continued up until 1993 when the base was finally closed down. Left to become derelict and overgrown, the complex provided an excellent environment for the police firearms team to carry out tactical training days. Some of the abandoned Nissan huts were in the same condition as they had been in 1945, with posters of voluptuous pin-up girls on the walls and even tin coffee mugs left undisturbed for almost half a century. In recognition of the town's numerous links with the United States, it is twinned with Lake County, Illinois.

Twenty-first-century Warrington is a bustling town with a growing population, a thriving business community, and a vibrant night life. Bordering the huge conurbations of Liverpool and Manchester it was a challenging policing environment, where home grown and travelling criminals kept me and my colleagues fully occupied.

As a uniformed chief inspector, my role was managerial, working with Nick and the team to deliver effective policing within our limited budget. I did have some opportunity to return to my roots as an operational cop, and that was when I was at my happiest.

Technology had improved greatly by 2004, and the morning briefing was a divisionwide affair with a video link across the six police stations which made up Northern Area. When I chaired my first video briefing, it took a little getting used to. It was slightly reminiscent of the Eurovision Song Contest, and I felt like Terry Wogan greeting the presenter in Reykjavik and asking for the votes of the Icelandic jury.

Each morning we examined the twenty-four-hour crime

return, highlighted notable incidents, and planned our tactics for the day. We discussed significant arrests and allocated resources to deal with prisoners. It was an exciting, dynamic environment, and I felt immense satisfaction that after all these years, I still enjoyed coming to work.

"I've been looking at your operational order for the Christmas public order patrols, Griff," said Nick. "What d'you want me to do?"

"You're the boss, Nick – what d'you want to do?" I asked.

"Why don't you and I do one of the night shifts together, foot patrol Warrington town centre. It'd be better than this lark," he said, glancing around his office.

"Sounds good to me," I said.

The build-up to Christmas is always a testing time when resources are stretched to the limit. I had been given the task of drawing up a series of special initiatives to put extra staff in the town centres of Warrington, Widnes, and Runcorn to deal with the mindless, drunken violence which traditionally accompanies the season of goodwill. By changing some shift patterns, bringing in volunteer special constables, and utilising community support officers, we had the makings of a credible team sheet, to which I added Nick and myself.

After taking the night shift briefing in Warrington's huge parade room, I headed to Nick's office.

"What d'you reckon?" asked Nick, resplendent in full uniform and body armour.

"Very smart, Sir," I offered.

The town centre was packed and spirits were high as Nick and I wandered the streets chatting to revellers, shaking hands, and even accepting kisses on the cheek from a hen party clearly not dressed for the weather. It wasn't long before the good-natured partying turned sour, as a disagreement outside a nightclub developed into a free-for-all.

"Assistance required outside Mr Smith's. Patrols to acknowledge?"

"Chief Inspector, en route."

Nick and I sprinted to the scene of the disturbance, where a young PC had pinned a man face down in the street and was struggling to get handcuffs on him. With my help, we soon had him under control, as Nick intervened between two other men who were about to start throwing punches.

Blood, broken glass, foul and abusive language – and not an e-mail in sight. Wonderful!

Outside another bar, a young man was lying face up on the pavement and shaking violently, apparently in the throes of a major fit. Nick and I pushed our way through the crowd, and I took hold of the man's head to prevent him injuring himself.

Nick radioed for an ambulance as two of our colleagues began questioning onlookers and taking names and addresses. We had no idea what had gone on and couldn't rule out the possibility that the young man had been assaulted. As I held his head he continued to shake, his eyes rolling back so that only the whites were visible. Within minutes a paramedic was on the scene, injecting adrenaline into a vein in an attempt to stabilise the patient.

I suspected that the man had sustained a serious head injury, one which could prove fatal, so as the paramedic went about his business, Nick and I began cordoning the area off as a crime scene. A second paramedic arrived and immediately called me over.

"I think I know this guy," he said. "If I'm right, he's got a small bird tattooed on his left ankle."

We both knelt down to take a look, and sure enough, there it was. A small Liver bird with the letters LFC underneath it.

"There's absolutely nothing wrong with him," said the ambulance man. "He's a Munchausen fitter."

I was unclear what the man's occupation had to do with it. I have a friend who is an engine fitter, and he doesn't behave like this.

"This is how he gets his kicks. He finds a busy place, lies down, and pretends to be fitting. I've dealt with him three times. He spends a night in hospital, gets up, and goes home. He loves it."

On the strength of this information, we scaled down the murder enquiry but still took as many names as possible just in case. Like me, you may be wondering how anyone could possibly consider lying on the cold, damp pavement shaking violently on a freezing December evening to be recreational activity, but hey, don't knock it till you've tried it.

The night shift wore on and the novelty wore off, and at five in the morning Nick and I headed back to the warmth of his office for a much-needed cup of tea.

Throughout my police service I had always felt the need to set myself new challenges, to seek new horizons. Every two or three years I needed to do something different, whether it be a new specialisation, a new station, or a step up the promotional ladder. Many of my friends and colleagues didn't share this urge and were happy to find their favoured role and stick to it, but that was never for me. As 2006 drew to a close, I was once again facing a watershed in my career, and this time I had a fourth option to add to my list of choices: retirement.

In March 2007 I would have thirty years service and could walk away with a reasonably comfortable pension. At fifty-two years of age I was under no obligation to go and could choose to stay for another eight years. If I did decide to stay on, I could maybe go for promotion to superintendent, either in Cheshire or elsewhere in the country. Perhaps I could try my luck overseas; there were opportunities to work in places such as Bosnia or Iraq at the time, and the idea did appeal to me. I have never been one to seek the views of others when faced with these types of decisions, preferring to rely on my own instincts, so Sally made no attempt to influence me. However, this was a bigger dilemma than I had faced before, and I did experience a degree of uncertainty. The gentle steer which I needed came out of the blue in the form of a letter from June Whitfield. You may remember her as the comedy actress who appeared in many TV sitcoms during the seventies and eighties, notably *Terry and June* in which she starred alongside Terry Scott. Let me explain: I do not know June personally, not even as a pen friend. The letter in question was a promotional circular advertising funeral plans, and it fell through my letter box one morning just as I was on my way out to work.

"Are you aged fifty to eighty?" it said alongside a picture of a man who looked at least one hundred. I had never before considered myself to be in the fifty-to-eighty group. It wasn't that long ago that I routinely received mail from Club 18/30 Holidays seeking to tempt me with the thinly veiled promise of sun, sea, and sex – now I was being asked to choose between burial or cremation. June was suggesting to me that now was the time to think about these things and that for as little as one pound a week I could secure my big day at today's prices, thus beating inflation.

Included with the letter were several leaflets advertising things such as incontinence pants, an ultraviolet machine for cleaning dentures, support stockings, and that mode of transport loved by incontinent octogenarians the world over – the Stenna Stair Lift. Clearly, my membership of Club 50/80 had opened up a whole new world for me.

"Look at this, Sal," I said.

Sally stared long and hard at the letter, a look of concerned concentration on her face.

"So what do you think?" she said.

"Regarding?" I asked.

"Burial or cremation."

"Surprise me!" I said in exasperation, dashing out of the door clutching a piece of toast.

June's letter had a profound effect on me. It brought home to me that I was no longer a young man and that I was now closer to the Grim Reaper than to the midwife. I may not be ready for the incontinence pants and ultraviolet ray gun just yet, but I wasn't getting any younger. By the time I arrived at my office, my mind was made up; I would complete the retirement notification form, thus giving the force three months' notice, and I would give some thought to what I intended to do with the rest of my life.

I didn't sign up for June's funeral plan, and on the subject of burial or cremation, the jury's still out.

CHAPTER 9

Journey's End

6 March 2007

I sat in my office at Runcorn Police Station and looked around the room. For some months I had anticipated this day and wondered how I would feel on my last day as a police officer. I had seen many friends pack up their kit on the final day of service, and several had been forced to suppress a tear. I was determined not to allow the emotion of the occasion get to me – but I was fearful that it might. In truth, I felt numbness rather than sadness and was confident that I would not be seen to shed a tear.

Having read and actioned my e-mails for the last time ever, I took two black bin sacks from the bottom drawer of my desk and began collecting together some personal items. Among them was a faded wooden, six-inch ruler with "PC 1002 Griffin" written on it in biro. This had been given to me thirty years before by Dave Jones when he was my tutor constable, and it had seen active service almost daily ever since. My mind skipped back to those early days and the impression Dave had made on me. I had, at that time, no burning desire to be promoted and not the slightest wish to become a chief inspector. My ambition then was, one day, to be as good a cop as Jonesey. Had I ever achieved that ambition? Probably not. In a plastic cube on my desk were dozens of business cards, including the one from Jeremy the spy, and an assortment of letters and reports which I felt unable to confine to the shredder. Each item was carefully examined before being placed reverently in the sack ready for the journey to its new home in my attic. I then began removing the framed photographs and certificates from the walls. There were team and class pictures from an assortment of events and training courses, each one holding very personal memories of people, places, and times past. There was a French Foreign Legion calendar given to me by a former Legionnaire whom I'd once met in Germany, a picture of my wife and children, and finally a photo of the other great love of my life – Tranmere Rovers Football Club.

Having placed all my worldly possessions just outside my office door, I went to say a last farewell to Denise. As I walked into her office, she stopped typing and stood up from behind her desk. Four feet eleven inches of unparalleled efficiency and unswerving loyalty, Denise had been my guardian angel for many years. She had managed my post, booked train tickets, arranged hire cars, and when necessary, counselled me over coffee. She had answered my phone, often resolving the issue herself, dealt with cold callers to my office, and had shielded me from harm.

"I'm pretty much done now, Dee," I said as I walked towards her. "I'm going to call it a day."

No further words were spoken as we hugged, nor were any necessary. My lower lip began to quiver, and for a moment I feared that I was about to blubber in a very un—chief inspector fashion. I was going to miss Denise, and I suspected that the feeling was mutual.

Grabbing my two bin bags, I headed off along the corridor and down the stairs at the back of the nick. I felt no desire to tour the building, saying goodbye and squeezing hands; maybe I should have. It was an incredibly private moment, and I was alone with my thoughts and my memories.

I placed my gear in the boot of my car and took one last look around the station yard. I remembered the many times Peter and I strolled around it while discussing divisional business, affairs of state, and sometimes football. I remembered Max approaching me on my first day as a newly promoted sergeant and asking if I knew where the vacuum cleaner was. I remembered violent prisoners being hauled from patrol cars and manhandled into the lift en route to the cells above. I remembered laughter, shouting, swearing, sirens, and blue lights. Now, however, all was quiet as I sat in my car and prepared to leave for the last time.

The automatic security gates slowly parted as I drove towards them and out into the street. In my rear-view mirror I saw them close behind me, silently signalling the end of my thirty-year journey. It was then that the tears came.

The End

Epilogue

The lights of Nerja town twinkled in the distance as the sun set over the Mediterranean. It was an idyllic scene, and I felt relaxed and contented as I sipped my gin and tonic on the balcony. Ever since reading Hemingway's _Death in the Afternoon_ all those years ago, I had had a love for Spain in general and for Andalusia in particular. On this occasion I had come to spend a few days alone, gathering my thoughts and considering my future. It was only four days since I had relinquished my warrant card and become a member of the public, and it would be some time yet before I would get used to the idea that I was no longer a cop.

I reflected on how the last thirty years had affected me as a person. Probably not greatly was my conclusion. I had seen some terrible things and had met some deeply unpleasant people, but I had not given way to hatred. I still believe that the overwhelming majority of people are basically decent and that there is some decency in even the worst of us.

I remembered some of the many people I'd worked with over the last thirty years and how my life had been enriched by the experience. Someone once said, "Judge a man not by how much money he earns but by how many friends he has," and in that regard I consider myself extremely fortunate. I would be hard pressed to put a number to my list of friends, but I like to think that I have made very few enemies during my journey.

I thought about my family and considered myself very lucky

to have the love of my wife and children. I thought about those I had lost: my mother, Margaret and Don, and my ex–wife, Mary, who died after a long illness in 2006.

I wondered what I would do with the rest of my life and whether I should embark on some other journey; at fifty-two years of age there was still time. Some other career, voluntary work maybe, who knows. I had always enjoyed writing; maybe I could write a book. Probably not.

I could certainly devote more time to my family now, and with a ten-year-old son and a six-year-old daughter, as well as a nineteen-year-old daughter from my first marriage, maybe that would be enough to fill my days for a few years.

It was probably too early to make these decisions, so for the time being I contented myself with the view, the warm Mediterranean air, and the gin.

Hasta Luego Mis Amigos

PS: The vacuum cleaner is in the small cupboard next to the property store.

Murder Enquiry – Leslie Guntripp

The brutal murder of Mr Leslie Guntripp at Winsford in February 1978 remains undetected to this day. If you have any information about this or any other crime please contact Cheshire Police on

0845 458 0000.

Alternatively, information can be passed anonymously via the Crimestoppers Hotline on 0800 555 111.

Lightning Source UK Ltd.
Milton Keynes UK
UKOW051804221211

184288UK00001B/4/P